Plato: How Philosophy Shapes Human Understanding.

Philosophical compendiums, Volume 2

Rodrigo v. santos

Published by Pomar Assets, 2025.

While every precaution has been taken in the preparation of this book, the publisher assumes no responsibility for errors or omissions, or for damages resulting from the use of the information contained herein.

PLATO: HOW PHILOSOPHY SHAPES HUMAN UNDERSTANDING.

First edition. February 1, 2025.

Copyright © 2025 Rodrigo v. santos.

ISBN: 979-8230844020

Written by Rodrigo v. santos.

Table of Contents

Who Was Plato: 1
Introduction: 2
1st Tetralogy 4
Alcibiades 5
Lysis 10
Laques 15
Charmides 20
2nd Tetralogy 27
Protagoras 28
Hippias Minor 35
Greater Hippias 42
Gorgias 47
3rd Tetralogy 51
Meno 52
Euthyphro 57
The Apology of Socrates 64
Crito 69
4th Tetralogy 75
The Symposium 76
Phaedrus 82
The Republic 88
Phaedo 95
5th Tetralogy 102
Cratylus 103
Ion 110
Euthydemus 115
Menexenus 122
6th Tetralogy 127
Parmenides 128

Theaetetus	136
The Sophist	141
Political	146
7th Tetralogy	154
Philebus	155
Timaeus	161
Critias	169
Laws	175
Final Notes:	180
Bibliographic references:	181

"I would first like to dedicate this work to my beloved savior, who watches over all of us, and to the teams that created all the digital tools necessary for the production of this and many other wonderful works. My gratitude to you all."

Who Was Plato:

Aristocles (with the name Plato being merely a nickname) was an ancient Greek philosopher who lived around 427/428 BCE to 347/348 BCE. He is widely considered one of the most influential thinkers in the history of Western philosophy and was a disciple of Socrates, another notable Greek philosopher. Plato founded the Academy of Athens, one of the first higher education institutions in history, where he passed on his teachings to a group of students, including the famous philosopher Aristotle.

Plato is known for his philosophical dialogues, in which he explored a wide range of topics, including ethics, politics, epistemology, metaphysics, and the theory of knowledge. His philosophical thought is often presented through characters, with Socrates frequently being the protagonist of his dialogues. Some of Plato's most well-known dialogues include *The Republic*, *Phaedrus*, and *The Apology of Socrates*.

Among Plato's most influential ideas is the theory of forms or ideas, which suggests that the visible world is merely a shadow or imperfect imitation of the eternal and perfect world of ideas. He also emphasized the importance of justice and education in building a just society. His writings continue to be studied and debated in contemporary philosophy and have had a lasting impact on the Western philosophical tradition.

Introduction:

Plato's works, especially his seven Tetralogies, represent some of the most important milestones in Western philosophy. However, their complexity and richness of content can become barriers for many readers seeking to understand his central ideas. The purpose of this ebook is precisely to facilitate this understanding by offering a literary analysis that simplifies what may initially seem like a labyrinth of profound and often challenging concepts.

Here, we aim to present an accessible approach to Plato's philosophical discussions, simplifying the dialogues and highlighting their most relevant questions: the nature of justice, the pursuit of true knowledge, criticism of politics and society, as well as reflections on the human soul and reality. Our goal is not only to explain the works clearly but also to inspire the reader with a new perspective on themes that remain deeply relevant in contemporary philosophy.

Whether you are a student, a curious reader, or someone seeking to deepen your understanding of Plato, this compendium offers a reading that brings his philosophy closer and makes it more comprehensible. With clarity and precision, we strive to translate Plato's complex discussions into something more straightforward and accessible, without losing sight of the depth that characterizes the great Athenian thinker.

From here, we invite you to explore Plato's dialogues in a new and enriching way, with the hope of making his philosophy more relevant to our daily lives and our understanding of the world.

1st Tetralogy

Alcibiades

"Alcibiades," part of the first tetralogy of Platonic dialogues, stands out not only for the depth of its ideas but also for the skillful way in which Plato constructs his argument and addresses essential philosophical questions. This dialogue is a true *tour de force* in the tradition of Greek philosophy and continues to be widely studied and debated over the centuries.

One of the first notable characteristics of *Alcibiades* is its dialogical nature. Plato, a master of the philosophical dialogue, uses the conversation between Socrates and Alcibiades to examine the idea of self-awareness and self-knowledge. Through a series of questions and answers, Socrates challenges Alcibiades to examine his own soul and recognize his ignorance. This Socratic method of questioning is one of the most distinctive elements of Platonic philosophy, and *Alcibiades* demonstrates it brilliantly.

Another remarkable aspect of this dialogue is the way Plato addresses the issue of government and leadership. Alcibiades was a prominent figure in 5th-century BC Athens, and the work raises important questions about the relationship between philosophical knowledge and the ability to govern. Socrates argues that the true ruler must be someone who possesses knowledge and wisdom, rather than merely seeking power for its own sake. This idea has profound implications not only for politics but also for ethics and education.

A recurring theme in *Alcibiades* is the pursuit of self-knowledge. Plato argues that the first step to becoming a wise and virtuous leader is to know oneself. Socrates challenges Alcibiades to examine his beliefs and values, question his actions, and seek inner truth. This process of self-examination is a journey that Plato emphasizes in many of his dialogues, and *Alcibiades* is no exception.

The richness of language and the depth of ideas in *Alcibiades* make it a captivating work worthy of continued study. Plato masterfully uses dialogue as a tool to explore complex philosophical issues in an accessible and engaging way. His arguments are often intricate and challenging, but he presents them clearly and persuasively, making *Alcibiades* a dialogue that captivates readers from beginning to end.

Moreover, *Alcibiades* offers a rare insight into Socratic philosophical pedagogy, highlighting his unique method of questioning and provocation. The relationship between Socrates and Alcibiades is complex, with Socrates acting as a guide seeking to direct the young leader in his quest for self-knowledge. This relationship exemplifies the role of the philosopher in Ancient Athens, who not only conveyed knowledge but also helped interlocutors reflect and question their own beliefs.

Another noteworthy feature of *Alcibiades* is how Plato explores the nature of desire and ambition. Alcibiades is portrayed as someone with unrestrained political ambitions but lacking a deep understanding of himself. Socrates points out the difference between the desire for power and the desire for wisdom, emphasizing the importance of directing our impulses constructively and reflecting on our true motivations.

This aspect of the dialogue resonates not only in politics but also in everyday life, where the pursuit of success often overshadows the search for authenticity and wisdom. Plato's writing in *Alcibiades* is a remarkable example of clarity and elegance. His dialogues are like an intricate puzzle of words, where each piece fits perfectly into the next, forming a cohesive whole. His ability to express complex ideas in an accessible manner is one of the reasons why his works continue to be widely read and studied, even after more than two millennia.

The influence of *Alcibiades* on philosophy and political theory is undeniable. The issue of self-knowledge and the pursuit of wisdom remains a central theme in contemporary philosophy. Furthermore, the notion that leadership should be based on the search for truth and ethical reflection remains relevant in a world where power is often obtained and exercised opportunistically.

What is even more intriguing about *Alcibiades* is how Plato transcends purely political questions and delves into the complexities of the human soul. The dialogue leads us to question not only the role of philosophy in shaping leaders but also how philosophy can be a path to self-reflection and personal transformation. The timeless nature of *Alcibiades* is evident when we look at the contemporary world. In an era where politics often seems driven by selfish interests and power is frequently sought without a real commitment to truth and virtue, the lessons of *Alcibiades* remain deeply relevant.

Plato reminds us that authentic leadership requires deep introspection, a commitment to the pursuit of wisdom, and honesty with oneself that transcends political conveniences. Furthermore, Plato's writing in *Alcibiades* demonstrates his exceptional ability to create captivating characters and engaging dialogues. Through Socrates' eloquence and Alcibiades' initial reluctance to confront his own limitations, the reader is immediately drawn into a conversation that unfolds like a philosophical drama, full of intellectual twists and profound revelations. Plato's mastery of rhetoric and argumentation is evident in every line.

Beyond philosophical questions, *Alcibiades* also sheds light on the culture and society of Ancient Greece, offering readers a fascinating window into the past. The political and moral concerns discussed in the dialogue are deeply rooted in the culture of the time, and Plato provides us with a glimpse into the complexities and contradictions of ancient Athens.

On a broader level, *Alcibiades* is not just a philosophical dialogue but also a mirror of human complexity. Through Alcibiades' doubts and hesitations, we see the universal conflict between unrestrained ambition and the search for deeper meaning in life. Plato's work challenges us to explore our own desires and aspirations, prompting us to question whether our goals are truly authentic and worthy.

Another captivating aspect of *Alcibiades* is how Plato shapes Socrates' character as a wise and provocative mentor. Socrates does not provide ready-made answers but instead guides Alcibiades to formulate his own responses, encouraging him to think deeply about his beliefs and actions. This demonstrates Socrates' fundamental belief in the importance of critical thinking and the inherent capacity of everyone to seek the truth.

It is remarkable how the dialogue *Alcibiades* continues to challenge and inspire philosophers, scholars, and readers from all walks of life. The fundamental questions it addresses—self-knowledge, leadership, ambition, and wisdom—are as relevant now as they were in ancient Athens. With each new reading and interpretation, new layers of meaning are unveiled, and Plato's reflections resonate in our time, inviting us to look within ourselves and at the world with a more critical and perceptive eye.

In conclusion, *Alcibiades* is a captivating philosophical work that continues to challenge and inspire readers across generations. Its exploration of the complexities of the human soul, the relationship between power and knowledge, and the pursuit of wisdom remain as relevant today as they were in Plato's time. Reading *Alcibiades* is an intellectual journey, an adventure that takes us to the depths of self-knowledge and invites us to reflect on the true meaning of wisdom and excellence. This timeless dialogue is a testament to the richness of philosophical thought and Plato's ability to guide us through the complexities of human existence with grace and depth.

Lysis

The work *Lysis* by Plato is a magnificent addition to the first tetralogy of the illustrious Greek philosopher. This work, a true treasure of ancient philosophy, offers us a profound reflection on friendship and the nature of the soul. With his masterful prose, Plato guides us through an engaging and thought-provoking dialogue that prompts us to question our own conceptions of friendship and the pursuit of truth.

The dialogue begins with Socrates and his young interlocutors, Lysis and Menexenus, exploring the theme of friendship. Amid an apparently casual conversation, Plato leads us on a philosophical journey in which we are invited to reflect on the nature of friendship and its implications in the search for self-knowledge. Through Socrates' insightful questioning, we explore the different forms of friendship, highlighting their complexities and subtleties.

The dialogue demonstrates how friendship can be a path to self-knowledge and the realization of our true nature. As the conversation unfolds, Plato presents his characteristic ability to reveal the contradictions and ambiguities of our beliefs and conceptions. He challenges us to reflect on the nature of friendship, showing how it is often based on selfish interests or temporary conveniences. With mastery, he makes us realize that true friendship is not limited to material interests or a mere exchange of favors but is a bond that transcends personal interest, rooted in the pursuit of wisdom and virtue.

Furthermore, *Lysis* also invites us to explore the nature of the soul. Plato introduces the idea that friendship is an expression of the affinity of souls and encourages us to reflect on the relationship between friendship and self-knowledge. He demonstrates how friendship can be a means of discovering our own essence since, by knowing our friend, we also come to know ourselves. This connection between friendship and the pursuit of truth is one of the key contributions of this dialogue to philosophy.

In *Lysis*, Plato once again demonstrates his mastery of the art of philosophical dialogue. His ability to lead the reader through deep and engaging reflection is truly remarkable. He challenges us to question our beliefs and conceptions about friendship and the nature of the soul, urging us to seek a deeper understanding of ourselves and the world around us. Throughout the dialogue, Plato invites us to consider the importance of intellectual humility and constant questioning. Socrates, with his posture as an eternal learner, teaches us that true friendship is not just about reinforcing our own opinions but about allowing a friend to challenge us, confront us, and help us grow. This reminds us that philosophy is a continuous process of self-discovery and expansion of thought, and friendship can be a valuable instrument in this process.

Another captivating aspect of *Lysis* is how Plato explores the relationship between youth and wisdom. The young characters, Lysis and Menexenus, bring with them a vibrant energy and a genuine desire to seek the truth. Socrates, with his experience and insight, guides them with patience and wisdom, showing that the pursuit of truth is not a privilege of the older but a path that anyone can follow, regardless of age. This dynamic between youth and experience reminds us of the importance of intergenerational dialogue in the pursuit of knowledge.

The narrative of *Lysis* also invites us to reflect on the complexity of language and communication. Throughout the dialogue, the characters often discover that seemingly simple words conceal profound and often ambiguous meanings. This makes us question our own ability to understand and express our thoughts and feelings, emphasizing the importance of clear and open communication in building authentic relationships.

Moreover, *Lysis* highlights the idea that true friendship is a journey of self-transformation. As the characters explore the meaning of friendship, they are confronted with their own limitations and contradictions. They realize that true friendship requires self-knowledge and authenticity and that the pursuit of wisdom is inseparable from the pursuit of virtue. This emphasis on personal transformation and the search for virtue makes *Lysis* a work of rare philosophical depth and relevance.

The richness of *Lysis* lies not only in the profound exploration of friendship and the nature of the soul but also in how Plato incorporates literary and philosophical elements that make the dialogue a masterpiece of rhetoric and dialectics. The philosopher's skill in creating lively and engaging characters, representing different aspects of society and the pursuit of knowledge, is remarkable. Each character has a distinct voice and plays a crucial role in building the argument, turning the dialogue into a theatrical piece that captivates the reader.

The use of metaphors and analogies in *Lysis* is another impressive aspect. Plato employs vivid and poetic imagery to illustrate complex concepts, making philosophy accessible and visually impactful. He invites us to think of friendship as a kind of affinity between souls, comparable to a musical harmony that transcends mere superficial interaction. These metaphors not only enrich the reading experience but also lead us to delve deeper into the philosophical issues being explored.

One of the most striking moments in *Lysis* is the relentless pursuit of a definition of friendship. The characters, guided by Socrates, attempt to find a definitive answer to the question: what is friendship? However, the answer remains elusive, and Plato leads us to question whether the true nature of friendship can ever be fully captured in a precise definition. This relentless quest for clarity and precision in defining concepts is a distinctive feature of Platonic philosophy, and *Lysis* exemplifies it remarkably.

The dialogue culminates in a profound lesson about self-knowledge and authenticity. Plato reminds us that true friendship and the pursuit of wisdom are intrinsically linked to self-reflection and the acceptance of our own limitations. He challenges us to be honest with ourselves and others, to recognize our biases, and to be willing to revise our beliefs in the search for truth. This message resonates powerfully in a world where superficiality and false authenticity often prevail.

Lysis, an essential part of Plato's first tetralogy, is a dialogue that transcends mere philosophical reflection; it flows like a winding river through the hearts and minds of its readers, provoking deep inquiry into the complexities of friendship and the nature of the human soul. In its simplicity, Plato presents a narrative that, like a mirror, reflects the countless nuances of friendship, challenging us to question what it truly means to be a friend and the intrinsic nature of human relationships.

Ultimately, *Lysis* is a vivid and engaging exploration of friendship, the soul, and the search for truth. The dialogue resonates through the centuries, challenging us to question and deepen our understanding of our relationships and the nature of friendship. It is a masterful demonstration of Plato's ability to combine philosophical depth with captivating narrative, continuing to inspire and provoke readers worldwide.

Laques

"*L aques*," by Plato, is a work that stands out as one of the philosophical gems of the first tetralogy of the Greek master. In this dialogue, Plato guides us through a profound and engaging reflection on the virtue of courage, exploring not only its fundamental characteristics but also its impact on the construction of human identity and society. The text is a testament to Plato's philosophical genius and his ability to create engaging dialogues rich in meaning.

Through a conversation between Socrates and two young Athenians, Laques and Nicias, Plato leads us on a fascinating exploration of courage and its role in an individual's life. Laques, a young athlete seeking to enhance his courage, and Nicias, a promising young man, form the perfect backdrop to investigate courage in its various facets. Through their responses and dialogues, Plato offers us a deep yet accessible analysis of the qualities of courage.

What makes *"Laques"* so captivating is Plato's ability to present solid arguments in an engaging and accessible manner. He not only explores philosophical concepts but also relates them to everyday life, making the work relevant and thought-provoking for any reader. It's as if we are sitting in ancient Athens itself, participating in the discussion and learning from the masters of philosophy. Furthermore, the work also addresses timeless questions about the nature of courage and its importance. Plato makes us question what it means to be courageous and how courage relates to virtue and character. He prompts us to reflect on how courage can be applied in different areas of life, from the political sphere to the personal decisions we face daily.

Another aspect that deserves attention is Plato's ability to create vivid and engaging characters. Laques and Nicias are not mere spectators in the narrative but individuals with distinct personalities and opinions. Their interactions with Socrates reveal not only the depth of their convictions but also the complexity of courage as a virtue. These characters contribute to the richness of the dialogue, making it even more compelling.

"Laques" is a work that, although written over two thousand years ago, maintains its relevance and impact. Courage continues to be a fundamental virtue in our lives, and the reflections presented by Plato are timeless. The way he addresses the issue of courage, linking it to human character and society, is a testament to the genius of the Greek philosopher.

The beauty of Platonic philosophy lies in its ability to transcend time and space, offering us profound insights that continue to resonate in our lives. In *"Laques,"* Plato not only discusses courage but also the relationship between courage and wisdom. He leads us to consider whether courage without wisdom is truly virtuous. This intricate issue is explored through the insightful dialogue between Socrates and his young interlocutors, guiding us on a philosophical journey of discovery.

The dialogue begins with Laques and Nicias seeking advice on how to cultivate courage in their lives. Socrates, the master of irony and philosophical inquiry, challenges them to think more deeply about what it means to be courageous. He encourages them to question whether courage, detached from wisdom, is merely a reckless disposition devoid of moral value. This interplay between courage and wisdom is a theme that resonates throughout Plato's work and is particularly intriguing in *"Laques."*

The captivating review cannot overlook Plato's rhetorical brilliance. His dialogues are like intellectually stimulating theatrical performances, where words are the main actors. He shows us that philosophy doesn't have to be hermetic or inaccessible but can be alive, dynamic, and fascinating. Through persuasive arguments and real-world examples, Plato engages the reader, challenging them to question their own beliefs and explore the meaning of courage in their own lives.

As the dialogue progresses, Plato also leads us to a profound reflection on education and the formation of character. He argues that true courage cannot be achieved through artificial means, such as the mere repetition of physical exercises. Instead, courage is intrinsically linked to wisdom and an understanding of the consequences of our actions. This is a timeless lesson that resonates in our contemporary pursuit of meaningful education and personal development.

"*Laques*" is a work that challenges us to examine not only courage but also the nature of virtue itself. Plato makes us consider whether courage is the first and most important of all virtues or if it is merely a part of a larger picture of virtuousness. His questions and arguments prompt us to think deeply about how we build our character and how we live a virtuous life.

The greatness of Plato's "*Laques*" lies in its ability to transcend time and deeply engage with the core of universal human issues. By addressing courage and wisdom, Plato sheds light on a dilemma that continues to resonate in our modern lives. His exploration of the relationship between courage and wisdom encourages us to consider whether courage without wisdom is truly virtuous or if, on the contrary, true courage can only flourish when accompanied by an understanding of the consequences of our actions. This intricate and timeless theme takes us on a journey of self-knowledge and reflection that is captivating in its depth.

As the dialogue unfolds, we are reminded of Plato's rhetorical and dialectical skill. His dialogues are like intellectual spectacles, where words take center stage. He shows us that philosophy doesn't need to be dry or hermetic; instead, it can be alive, dynamic, and fascinating. Through insightful arguments and real-life examples, Plato engages the reader in a dance of ideas, challenging them to question their own beliefs and explore the meaning of courage in their own existence. "*Laques*" challenges us to examine not only courage but also the very nature of virtue. Plato makes us question whether courage is the first and most important of all virtues or if it is merely a piece of a larger puzzle of virtuousness. His questions and arguments encourage us to reflect deeply on how we build our character and how we live a virtuous life in a complex and ever-evolving world.

Ultimately, Plato's *"Laques"* is a work that reminds us that philosophy is timeless and that its fundamental questions continue to resonate through the centuries. Through an engaging dialogue and insightful arguments, Plato guides us on a journey of self-discovery and reflection that is captivating in its depth and relevance. This text is living proof that philosophy can be not only captivating but also a source of wisdom and understanding that transcends the boundaries of time and culture.

Charmides

"Charmides," one of Plato's works that is part of the first tetralogy, is an intriguing philosophical dialogue that transports us to the world of ancient Athens, where the philosopher Socrates leads a thought-provoking discussion on the nature of wisdom and temperance. This captivating and timeless text invites us to dive deep into Plato's philosophical reflections and challenges us to question our own conceptions of virtue and wisdom.

The work begins with Socrates meeting Charmides, a promising young man and distant relative of the famous Athenian legislator, Solon. Socrates is curious about the knowledge and wisdom Charmides may have acquired, and this curiosity triggers a series of fascinating dialogues about the virtue of temperance, which is central to Plato's reflection in "Charmides." The quest for a definition of temperance serves as a guiding thread throughout the dialogue, and the way Socrates approaches it, challenging the opinions of Charmides and other characters, is a masterful example of his Socratic method.

One of the remarkable features of this dialogue is Plato's ability to present complex arguments in an accessible way. He uses dialogues between Socrates and other characters to explore different perspectives and conceptions of temperance, allowing the reader to actively participate in the process of questioning and reflection. As the discussion progresses, we are led to question what it truly means to be temperate and how we can achieve this virtue in our lives. Additionally, "Charmides" offers a fascinating insight into the social and political relations of ancient Athens. The discussion of temperance is not approached in isolation, but in relation to the city-state, education, and the role of the youth in society. Through this dialogue, Plato makes us reflect on the importance of wisdom and temperance not only on an individual level but also as the foundations for a just and balanced society.

The dialogue "Charmides" is a work that challenges us to think deeply about essential questions of human existence. It encourages us to seek truth and wisdom, recognizing that the virtue of temperance is a constant journey of self-discovery and self-reflection. Through the words of Socrates and the engaging characters, Plato invites us to question our own conceptions of what wisdom is and how we can incorporate it into our lives. In the unending search for a definition of temperance, Plato uses the dialogue between Socrates and Charmides to explore not only the concept itself but also the nature of knowledge and self-awareness. As the conversation progresses, the characters reveal their own limitations and uncertainties, which leads us to question the true extent of our own understanding. This is a powerful reminder that wisdom is intrinsically tied to the recognition of our own ignorance, a fundamental principle of Socratic philosophy.

Plato also makes us reflect on the relationship between youth and wisdom. Charmides is a promising young man, and his name, associated with Solon's family, suggests historical weight and a heritage of virtue. However, throughout the dialogue, he is confronted with the complexity of temperance, and his youth and apparent inexperience come to the forefront. This leads us to consider how age and experience relate to wisdom, and whether virtue can truly be achieved without the passage of time and maturation. The structure of the dialogue is also noteworthy. Plato skillfully develops the narrative through the interaction between the characters, creating an intellectually stimulating debate environment. Each answer generates a new question, and each question takes us to a deeper level of reflection. This creates a sense of progression and discovery that keeps the reader engaged and eager for more.

Furthermore, "Charmides" is not limited to the abstract discussion of temperance. The dialogue explores the practical implications of virtue, examining how temperance manifests in daily actions and human relationships. This leads us to reflect on how philosophy should not only be a theoretical pursuit but also a guide for practical and moral life. However, Plato's work is not without ambiguities and challenges. The search for a clear and unequivocal definition of temperance remains unresolved at the end of the dialogue, leaving the reader with a sense of incompleteness. However, this openness to interpretation is a fundamental characteristic of Platonic philosophy, which encourages us to continue seeking answers and engaging in an ongoing intellectual dialogue.

The dialogue "Charmides" is not limited to the exploration of temperance and virtue but also presents a remarkable exploration of the Socratic dialectic, a method of questioning and philosophical investigation that became a landmark in the history of philosophy. As Socrates and his interlocutors discuss temperance, we are presented with a masterful sample of how Socratic philosophy operates. Socrates does not seek to impose ready-made answers but to guide his dialogue companions through a process of self-discovery and self-examination. This transformative approach is a valuable lesson for all seekers of truth, highlighting the importance of critical questioning and open dialogue in the search for knowledge. Another notable aspect of this dialogue is the way Plato leads us to question traditional notions of wisdom and authority. Charmides, though young and seemingly inexperienced, is treated with respect and consideration by Socrates, who recognizes the importance of listening and learning from all sources, regardless of age or social position. This challenges the social conventions of the time and leads us to consider how wisdom can be found in the most unexpected sources.

The richness of "Charmides" also lies in how Plato weaves political and ethical elements into his philosophical narrative. The dialogue does not take place in a vacuum but is rooted in the context of ancient Athens, a city-state deeply influenced by philosophy and politics. The search for temperance is not just a personal pursuit, but a search for the common good, for the harmony of the city, and for the improvement of society. This connection between philosophy and politics is a distinctive feature of Platonic philosophy and invites us to consider the importance of virtue not only for individuals but for society as a whole.

It is important to recognize that "Charmides" is a work that remains open to diverse interpretations. Plato himself, throughout his philosophical career, developed and deepened his ideas on temperance and virtue, making this work a fascinating piece in the puzzle of Platonic thought. This multiplicity of interpretations highlights the depth and complexity of Plato's philosophy and challenges us to continue exploring his works in search of ever-deeper insights and understandings. As we navigate the depths of the work "Charmides," we are prompted to contemplate the very nature of virtue and morality. Plato, through the dialogue between Socrates and his interlocutors, challenges us to reflect on whether temperance is an innate or acquired quality, whether it can be taught or learned, and whether it is a characteristic that endures throughout life or can be lost. These seemingly simple questions become complex as the characters explore the nuances of temperance, leaving us with the sense that virtue is an elusive quality that requires constant investigation and self-discipline.

Furthermore, "Charmides" is not without criticisms of Athenian society of its time. Socrates himself, through his incisive method of questioning, exposes the contradictions and limitations of conventional thought, often pointing to the lack of coherence between people's actions and words. Through his insightful approach, Plato raises questions about the nature of wisdom and morality in society, questioning whether social conventions are truly a reliable source of ethical guidance.

The dialogue "Charmides" also makes us reflect on the role of education in the formation of virtue. By discussing whether temperance can be taught, Plato leads us to consider how education plays a crucial role in shaping moral virtues. The idea that temperance can be passed down from one generation to another through teaching leads us to a broader reflection on the importance of education as a means of moral and civic improvement. However, it is important to note that Plato does not provide definitive answers but presents us with a series of philosophical questions that remain relevant and provocative to this day. This openness to interpretation and debate is one of the hallmarks of Platonic thought and one of the reasons why his works continue to captivate the minds and hearts of readers across time.

"Charmides," part of Plato's first tetralogy of dialogues, is a jewel of philosophy that continues to shine brightly even amidst the mists of time. In this work, Plato leads us through a labyrinth of inquiries and reflections, on an intellectual journey that profoundly and lastingly engages us. The dialogue between Socrates, Charmides, and other characters is, in itself, a representation of the essence of philosophical thought, which is the constant search to understand the nature of the world and the human being. What makes "Charmides" particularly fascinating is the way Plato chooses the theme of temperance as the central point of discussion. Temperance, or moderation, is a virtue that permeates everyone's daily life but is rarely analyzed in depth. In this dialogue, we are invited to unravel the mysteries of temperance, to question what it is, how it is acquired, and how we can recognize it in others and in ourselves. It is an exploration that takes us deep into the realms of morality, ethics, and human psychology.

One of the most captivating elements of this dialogue is the Socratic method. Socrates, in his relentless search for truth, uses careful questioning and irony to challenge the convictions of the dialogue's characters. He shows us that true wisdom cannot be found in dogmatic assertions, but in the willingness to question and examine our own beliefs. Through Socrates, Plato inspires us to embrace intellectual humility and to recognize that the search for wisdom is never finished, but rather a continuous journey. The richness of the work "Charmides" extends beyond the philosophical realm, also encompassing political and social issues in ancient Athens. The dialogue makes us reflect on the role of education in forming virtue, on how politics can be a field for the application of moral virtues, and on the importance of finding balance and harmony in public life.

Thus, Plato not only invites us to explore temperance as an individual virtue but also as a cornerstone for the construction of a just and balanced society. The true beauty of "Charmides" lies in its ability to transcend the boundaries of time and space. The questions Plato raises, Socrates' methods, and the complexities of virtue still resonate with contemporary humanity. It is a work that challenges us to question, reflect, deepen our knowledge, and seek wisdom and moderation in our own lives.

In conclusion, "Charmides" is an intellectually stimulating and spiritually enriching work that continues to captivate and inspire generations of thinkers, students, and curious minds. It is a reminder that philosophy is a journey that never ends, an endless search for truth, wisdom, and virtue. It is a work that invites us to enter the world of Platonic thought and lose ourselves in the meanders of philosophical inquiry, where the answers are never definitive, but the search is eternal.

2nd Tetralogy

Protagoras

"Protagoras," written by Plato as part of the second tetralogy, is a work that delves deeply into the issues of morality, knowledge, and virtue. In this philosophical dialogue, Plato presents us with a meeting between Socrates and Protagoras, the renowned sophist of ancient Greece. The title, which reflects the central figure of the narrative, invites us into a complex and captivating reflection on the limits of moral relativism and the quest for truth. Plato, known for his numerous contributions to philosophy, once again demonstrates his mastery in addressing crucial questions for humanity, keeping the reader eager for answers while also provoking a deep critique of the arguments presented.

At the core of the dialogue between Socrates and Protagoras lies the question of the nature of virtue and education. Protagoras maintains the idea that virtue can be taught, a bold statement that challenges the prevailing notion of the time. However, Socrates, always questioning and inquisitive, positions himself as a learner willing to explore the sophist's ideas. This leads us to a fascinating reflection on the role of knowledge in the formation of human character. The reader is prompted to ponder whether virtue is innate or acquired, whether it can be transmitted or must be earned through experience.

Plato's skill in creating engaging and persuasive dialogues is evident in "Protagoras." As the discussion unfolds, we are captivated by the characters' ability to articulate their ideas in a convincing and coherent manner. Through the interplay between Socrates and Protagoras, the author offers us a balanced view of different philosophical perspectives. This not only enriches the debate but also invites us to question our own beliefs and biases, making the reading a truly transformative experience.

In addition to the discussion of virtue and education, "Protagoras" also raises important questions about moral relativism. Protagoras asserts that "man is the measure of all things," implying that each individual defines their own truth and morality. This idea challenges concepts of objective truth and universal values. Once again, Socrates steps in, questioning this perspective and forcing the reader to reflect on the dangers of moral relativism. Through this discussion, Plato presents us with an intriguing moral dilemma that continues to resonate in contemporary philosophical debates.

"Protagoras," a brilliant dialogue by Plato in the second tetralogy, gifts us with a narrative that transcends its ancient origins. In this work, philosophy is elevated to an extraordinary level, guiding us through a maze of ideas, questions, and moral dilemmas that echo to this day. Like a beacon, the title guides us to the heart of philosophical discussion, throwing us into the epicenter of a clash of ideas that urges us to deeply reflect on the nature of virtue and truth.

Socrates and Protagoras, two giants of Greek philosophy, take center stage in this intriguing dialogue. The confrontation between these brilliant minds is a true duel of arguments, a battle of ideas where no one leaves unscathed. While Protagoras defends the position that virtue can be taught, Socrates challenges this notion, sowing doubt and raising fundamental questions about the nature of education and morality. Plato's mastery lies in his ability to immerse us in this conflict, making us feel like active participants in the discussions, witnessing the clash of perspectives, and absorbing every word with intense curiosity.

The issue of education is a guiding thread throughout the dialogue. The reader is confronted with the idea that virtue can be transmitted through instruction, a concept that challenges the prevailing beliefs of ancient Greece. As Socrates questions and investigates, we are led to a deep exploration of the roots of virtue and methods of teaching. This debate stimulates our minds and forces us to assess our own conceptions of education and character formation.

Plato, a master in the art of creating rich and engaging dialogues, presents us with a philosophical critique that is both challenging and inspiring. The characters are created with detail and depth, making the reading experience even more vivid. As Socrates and Protagoras explore moral and epistemological issues, we are prompted to question our own convictions and ponder the complexities of virtue and truth.

Another intriguing element of "Protagoras" is its approach to moral relativism. Protagoras proclaims that each individual is the measure of all things, implying that truth and morality are relative, varying from person to person. This idea, deeply challenging, places us before a fascinating moral dilemma. We are compelled to consider the implications of moral relativism and reflect on the existence of universal values. Through the dialogue between Socrates and Protagoras, Plato invites us to explore the tension between individual subjectivity and the objectivity of morality, throwing us into a journey of intellectual discovery.

The depth of the dialogue in "Protagoras" is not limited to the discussion of virtue, education, and moral relativism. Plato, with his insightful narrative, also sheds light on the importance of rhetoric and persuasion in the Greek society of the time. The figure of Protagoras, as a renowned sophist, represents the influence of eloquence and the power of words in shaping public opinion. The reader is confronted with the notion that skilled persuasion can shape reality in a powerful way, often challenging objective truth in favor of personal or political interests. Through this discussion, Plato invites us to critically examine rhetoric, emphasizing the importance of a constant search for truth in a world permeated by persuasive and often deceptive discourses.

The structure of the dialogue itself is a manifestation of Plato's talent. The characters are developed with depth and authenticity, and their voices stand out with distinct nuances. While Socrates seeks truth through dialogue and methodical inquiry, Protagoras represents confidence in the wisdom of rhetoric and persuasion. This duality of approaches places us before an intriguing philosophical dilemma and urges us to reflect on the nature of wisdom and knowledge. Plato's writing is engaging and rich in detail, creating a reading experience that transcends mere literary appreciation and becomes an immersive intellectual journey.

Moreover, "Protagoras" resonates with timeless relevance. The themes explored in this dialogue, such as the nature of knowledge, morality, education, and rhetoric, continue to challenge and inspire philosophers, scholars, and thinkers around the world. The clash between Socrates and Protagoras serves as a microcosm of contemporary philosophical debates, where the pursuit of truth, the relativity of morality, and the influence of rhetoric continue to be passionate topics of discussion. In this sense, "Protagoras" proves to be a timeless work that not only connects us with the distant past of ancient Greece but also compels us to confront the philosophical and ethical challenges of the present.

The breadth and depth of "Protagoras" transcend the limitations of space and time, revealing itself as a philosophical work that refuses to grow old. Through the dialogue between Socrates and Protagoras, Plato not only offers us an unparalleled view of classical Greek philosophy but also guides us through an exploration of universal human issues. Socrates' relentless questioning, his tireless quests for truth and wisdom, echo on every page as a call to the human mind to never cease investigating, to never take for granted answers that seem obvious, and to never stop fighting for deeper understanding.

Throughout this intellectual dialogue, "Protagoras" reveals itself as a multifaceted work that can be interpreted in various ways, challenging the reader to contemplate the many layers of meaning. Plato does not seek to provide easy answers, but rather to create a space for critical reflection. Through Socrates and Protagoras, he invites us to question the nature of virtue and education, to investigate the validity of moral relativism, and to explore the nuances of rhetoric. This openness to interpretation makes "Protagoras" a perpetually alive work, capable of adapting and evolving as readers delve into its rich philosophical terrain.

Additionally, the capacity of "Protagoras" to provoke endless dialogues and debates is undeniable. In our modern times, philosophy still grapples with questions similar to those Plato brought to the stage centuries ago. The ideas presented in this dialogue continue to challenge our understanding of the world, our value systems, and our quest for truth. The ability of "Protagoras" to transcend temporal and cultural boundaries and continue inspiring thinkers and philosophers is a testament to its enduring impact and unwavering importance in the philosophical tradition.

In summary, "Protagoras," included in Plato's second tetralogy, is a philosophical work that remains immersive, stimulating, and inspiring, even through the centuries. Its wealth of ideas, depth of characters, and ability to provoke critical thought are testaments to Plato's literary and philosophical genius. Reading this title is like entering a world where the quest for truth and the exploration of the complexities of morality and rhetoric never age, where each reading is an opportunity for deeper discovery and for a dialogue that spans the ages. "Protagoras" is, and will continue to be, a beacon that illuminates the path of philosophical reflection.

Hippias Minor

"Hippias Minor," one of the most enigmatic and intriguing works of the Greek philosopher Plato, is a dialogue that is part of the second tetralogy of his works. In this text, we will explore the depth and complexity of this work, which delves into issues of truth, knowledge, and rhetoric. With an engaging dialogue and iconic characters, Plato invites us to question what we really know and how we can distinguish truth from falsehood.

The plot of this dialogue is built around a conversation between Socrates and Hippias Minor, a renowned sophist and orator. Through a series of incisive questions, Socrates seeks to uncover Hippias's knowledge on a variety of topics, ranging from virtue to beauty. However, the dialogue reveals a fundamental tension between knowledge and rhetoric, as Hippias often responds with grandiose and eloquent statements that lack real substance. Through his masterful characterization of Socrates, Plato challenges the superficial and misleading view of rhetoric that is often accepted unquestioningly in society. He leads us to question the validity of pompous words and eloquent statements that often mask a lack of substantial knowledge. This insightful critique of rhetoric is as relevant today as it was in ancient Athens, where the ability to persuade often outweighed the pursuit of truth.

Furthermore, "Hippias Minor" also sheds light on the nature of knowledge. Socrates, with his Socratic approach of constant questioning, leads us to reflect on the extent of our own understanding and the limitations of what we know. This dialogue reminds us that knowledge should not be confused with the mere retention of information, but rather with the ability to seek truth and recognize our own intellectual limitations.

The work also emphasizes the importance of the constant pursuit of knowledge and intellectual humility. Plato, through Socrates, shows us that true wisdom lies in the awareness of our own ignorance. This lesson is timeless and encourages us to never stop seeking answers and to always question the assumptions that support our understanding.

The beauty of "Hippias Minor" lies not only in its ability to incite deep reflection but also in the way Plato uses eloquence and dialogue to stimulate the reader's mind. The Socratic method, characterized by incessant questioning, is the essence of this dialogue and becomes an invitation to the ongoing search for truth. Led by Socrates, readers are prompted to question not only Hippias's knowledge but also the very nature of rhetoric and argumentation.

As the conversation unfolds, it is impossible not to be impressed by Plato's skill in creating such vivid and convincing characters. Hippias Minor, with his self-confidence and impressive rhetoric, embodies the figure of the sophist that Plato frequently criticizes in his works. Socrates, on the other hand, emerges as the intellectual hero who, through incisive questions and logical argumentation, challenges preconceived notions and the superficiality of empty words.

The beauty of "Hippias Minor" also lies in how Plato distills complex philosophical questions into an accessible and engaging dialogue. He leads the reader to consider the broader implications of the issues raised, such as the relationship between knowledge and virtue, truth and eloquence, and the importance of seeking genuine wisdom amidst a sea of persuasive speeches.

One of the most notable features of this dialogue is the idea that virtue is intrinsically linked to knowledge. Socrates argues that in order to act virtuously, it is necessary to know what is right and wrong. This discussion deeply resonates with ethical and moral issues still debated today, demonstrating the timeless nature of Plato's philosophical reflections. "Hippias Minor" transcends the boundaries of time and space, remaining an intellectual beacon that continues to illuminate restless and curious minds around the world.

In this work, Plato not only challenges us to explore the complexities of rhetoric and knowledge but also to reflect on the nature of truth in a world permeated by persuasive and fallacious speeches. His characters, skillfully drawn, play such engaging roles that it is almost as if we are sitting in that ancient conversation room, watching an intellectual battle unfold before our eyes.

Socrates, with his intellectual humility and tireless thirst for knowledge, embodies the relentless pursuit of truth, regardless of the rhetorical tricks that may obscure it. He encourages us to question, to dig deeper, to not settle for appearances. And, through his dialogues with Hippias Minor, Plato leads us to a profound reflection on the intricate relationship between rhetoric and knowledge, a reflection that resonates as strongly in modern times as it did in classical Athens.

The plot of this dialogue, seemingly simple, is like an Ariadne's thread that leads us into the labyrinths of the human mind, where truths and illusions intertwine. Plato challenges us to question the validity of rhetoric, to point to the core of truth, which often hides under a layer of eloquence. Hippias Minor, with his persuasive art, exemplifies the figure of the sophist who prioritizes persuasion over truth, a figure that Plato frequently criticizes in his works.

The Socratic approach of questioning everything, of seeking authentic knowledge, not only sheds light on knowledge itself but also emphasizes the importance of virtue, which is inextricably linked to wisdom. The discussion of virtue and knowledge, central to "Hippias Minor," is one of the many areas in which Plato continues to challenge us, inciting reflections on ethics and morality, leading us to question our own understanding of these fundamental concepts.

As the reading progresses, it is difficult not to become involved in this relentless quest for truth, skillfully and cleverly guided by Plato and Socrates. The work inspires us not to simply accept ready-made truths but to investigate, question, and reflect critically. The dialogue invites us to embrace the journey of the human mind in search of wisdom, even when the ground is slippery and filled with rhetorical traps.

"Hippias Minor" is a deep dive into the ocean of rhetoric, truth, and knowledge, where the waters are turbulent, and philosophical questions spring forth like inexhaustible fountains. In this work by Plato, we are transported to ancient Athens, to the atmosphere filled with philosophical discussions and insightful dialogues, where Socrates, the master of irony, plays a central role in the search for truth. The richness of the dialogue is revealed in how Plato distills complex concepts into accessible words. He invites us to unravel the complex relationship between rhetoric and knowledge, exposing the seduction of eloquence, which often obscures the underlying truth. While Hippias Minor, the sophist who proudly wields his rhetorical skill, challenges elaborate arguments, Socrates relentlessly resists accepting empty statements and appeals for a deeper search for knowledge.

It is important to highlight how Plato, through this dialogue, also encourages us to examine the very process of searching for truth. Socrates, with his incisive questions and ability to expose ignorance, serves as a vivid reminder that the pursuit of knowledge is an ongoing journey, often filled with obstacles, such as the webs of rhetoric and intellectual arrogance. "Hippias Minor" urges us to embrace intellectual humility and recognize that true knowledge lies in the awareness of our own ignorance.

Another fascinating layer of this dialogue is the exploration of virtue as intrinsically linked to knowledge. The discussion on virtue and how it intertwines with knowledge is of such depth that it transcends time and remains relevant in our contemporary societies. Plato challenges us to consider how knowledge of what is right and wrong is fundamental to virtuous action, a reflection that echoes in crucial ethical and moral issues.

As we progress in reading "Hippias Minor," we are invited to enter a world of endless questioning, where the search for truth is a guiding thread that runs through the complex web of rhetoric and argumentation. Through Socrates, Plato inspires us not to simply accept statements passively but to investigate, doubt, and closely examine the claims made. We are challenged to deepen our understanding, not to settle for easy and superficial answers.

In conclusion, "Hippias Minor" is a work that transcends time and retains its relevance and intellectual appeal. The dialogue, with its vivid characters and deep exploration of the relationship between rhetoric and knowledge, remains an inspiration for all those who seek truth and wisdom. Plato gifts us with an intellectual gem that continues to shine brightly in the firmament of philosophy, guiding inquisitive minds through the ages, reminding us that the pursuit of knowledge and critical reflection are fundamental pillars of the intellectual journey and the search for truth.

Greater Hippias

"Greater Hippias" is a fascinating and challenging work by Plato, part of the second tetralogy, revealing itself as an engaging and profound read. This is a work that invites us to delve into the depths of Greek philosophical thought, exploring crucial questions about the nature of truth, knowledge, and rhetoric. From the perspective of this Socratic dialogue, Plato offers his readers a rich tapestry of ideas, woven with the argumentative skill of Socrates and Hippias, the central characters who unfold a brilliant intellectual dialogue.

The plot of this dialogue is quite intriguing, as it involves a meeting between Socrates and Hippias, a renowned sophist of the time. The setting is a rhetorical competition, where Hippias is invited to demonstrate his skills in the art of speaking and persuading. What unfolds from there is a clash of ideas, where Socrates not only questions Hippias's wisdom but also deepens the reflection on the nature of knowledge and truth. What makes "Greater Hippias" remarkable is the way Plato conducts the dialogue, using Socrates as his spokesperson to expose the hollow nature of sophistic rhetoric. In this context, Socrates acts as the detective of truth, questioning each statement made by Hippias and revealing his contradictions. This approach of Socrates, characterized by his irony and elenctic method, casts a revealing light on the pretensions of sophists in mastering the art of rhetoric.

However, what is most intriguing in this dialogue is how Plato examines the concept of truth and knowledge. The reader is invited to question what knowledge truly is and how we can distinguish truth from falsehood. Through Socrates' probing, we come to understand that knowledge cannot simply be reduced to the ability to speak persuasively, as the sophists argued. Instead, Plato makes us contemplate the idea that knowledge is the possession of true information and the ability to discern what is true from what is false. Through a series of paradoxes and complex arguments, Plato challenges us to reflect on the nature of knowledge, while questioning the validity of Hippias's claims. This leads us to a deeper analysis of the relationships between truth, rhetoric, and knowledge, which remains relevant and stimulating to this day.

"Greater Hippias" urges us to question our own beliefs and understand the importance of seeking truth with sincerity, rather than being swayed by superficial persuasion. "Greater Hippias" stands out for its intellectually challenging nature, as Socrates unfolds a complex game of questions and answers, leading Hippias into logical dead-ends that expose the limitations of his knowledge. The dialogue reaches its peak when Socrates questions Hippias about the definition of beauty, a central concept in Platonic philosophy. The ensuing discussion takes us into deep territory, where the concept of beauty is dissected and reexamined under a new and challenging light.

Plato's skill in weaving complex arguments and paradoxes into his prose is remarkable. He uses a variety of rhetorical techniques to guide the reader through the complexities of the dialogue, making the reading captivating and engaging. It is as though we are watching an intellectual game, where the minds of Socrates and Hippias collide, and we are invited to participate in this clash of ideas. The reader is forced to engage actively in the discussion, questioning and refining their own opinions as they progress through the reading.

Furthermore, "Greater Hippias" offers a rich view of Athenian society at the time. The rivalry between Socrates and the sophists reflects the philosophical and cultural tensions that permeated classical Athens. The sophists were considered by many to be manipulators of truth, while Socrates sought wisdom through dialogue and a sincere quest for truth. This historical and philosophical context adds an extra layer of depth to the dialogue, showing how issues of truth, knowledge, and rhetoric were crucial in ancient Athens.

The work, however, does not provide definitive answers, leaving the reader with more questions than answers. This is one of the trademarks of Plato's philosophy, which encourages us to continue the search for knowledge and truth. "Greater Hippias" is an invitation to critical thinking and deep reflection, a celebration of the philosophical process itself, where answers may be elusive, but the intellectual journey is enriching.

In "Greater Hippias," Plato offers a deep exploration of the nuances of language and rhetoric. This dialogue sheds incisive light on the human capacity to communicate and persuade, exposing the traps and limitations of language. Socrates, with his characteristic relentless questioning approach, reveals how words can be deceptive and how the mere ability to speak convincingly is not a reliable indicator of truth or wisdom. This makes us reflect on the contemporary relevance of this dialogue, especially in a world saturated with persuasive speech, fake news, and deceptive rhetoric.

Moreover, "Greater Hippias" challenges us to rethink our understanding of knowledge and truth. Plato, through Socrates, leads us to question whether it is possible to attain a true and solid understanding of any subject, and how we can distinguish genuine knowledge from mere sophistry. The emphasis on defining concepts, such as beauty, highlights the ongoing quest for essence and the reality underlying appearances. This search resonates with contemporary existential questioning, inviting us to probe the deeper layers of reality and question what is intrinsically valid.

At the heart of "Greater Hippias," Plato gifts us with a sharp analysis of the nature of excellence, truth, and rhetoric. As Socrates and Hippias engage in an intellectual duel, it becomes clear that the pursuit of truth is often a difficult and thorny task, full of traps and twists. Through the dialogue, we are invited to explore the distinction between appearance and reality, a theme that remains relevant in our era, marked by illusions and superficialities. Plato's ability to guide the reader through a maze of logical arguments, paradoxes, and imprecise definitions is remarkable. At each step, we are challenged to reflect on what it truly means to know and discern truth. As Socrates meticulously deconstructs Hippias's arguments, we are reminded that truth is not something that can be easily attained, but something that requires effort, introspection, and, above all, the courage to face uncertainty.

The issue of beauty, which prominently arises in the dialogue, plays a central role in the exploration of truth. What is beautiful? How can we define beauty universally? These are questions that challenge philosophical minds throughout history, and "Greater Hippias" immerses us in this relentless search for a deeper understanding of aesthetics and artistic appreciation.

Furthermore, the work invites us to reflect on the relationship between knowledge and intellectual humility. Socrates, by admitting his own ignorance and recognizing the complexity of philosophical issues, teaches us the importance of questioning our own beliefs and embracing the constant search for answers. This is a vivid reminder that the pursuit of truth is an ongoing process, requiring the willingness to confront uncertainty and relentlessly question our own convictions.

Through "Greater Hippias," Plato offers readers a rare opportunity to engage in a profound and captivating exploration of philosophical thought. This is an invitation to dive into the deep waters of philosophy, where the currents of thought flow vigorously, leading us to unforgettable intellectual challenges. It is a work that remains timeless, reminding us that issues of knowledge, truth, and rhetoric are eternal, and that the quest for understanding is a fascinating journey that should never cease.

Gorgias

Plato's *Gorgias* deserves a prominent place in the second tetralogy of the renowned Greek philosopher. This dialogue is part of a series of philosophical writings that explore the essence of rhetoric, morality, and justice, providing a deep and captivating insight into the nature of persuasion and the importance of the search for truth. Through a rich tapestry of dialogues between Socrates, Gorgias, and Polus, Plato leads us on a challenging intellectual journey that urges us to question our own understanding of rhetoric and virtue.

The dialogue begins with Socrates questioning Gorgias, a famous rhetorician, about the nature of his art and the ability to persuade. Here, Plato establishes the central issue that will be addressed throughout the work: the distinction between rhetorical persuasion and true conviction. As the conversation unfolds, we are confronted with the idea that rhetoric can be used to persuade, even when the speaker does not possess solid knowledge about the subject being discussed. This raises profound questions about the morality of rhetoric and its relationship to truth. The work also leads us to explore the concept of justice, a recurring theme in Plato's works. Socrates argues that justice is a form of knowledge and that the true rhetorician must seek justice in their words and actions. This leads us to reflect on the role of rhetoric in society and its ability to shape morality and justice.

What makes *Gorgias* so captivating is the way Plato guides the reader through a maze of arguments and counterarguments, challenging us to think critically about the nature of rhetoric and its relationship to truth. As Socrates questions Gorgias and his followers, we are prompted to question our own understanding of rhetoric and the importance of the pursuit of truth in our everyday communication. Furthermore, the work presents a unique view of the nature of wisdom and virtue. Plato argues that true wisdom is linked to the pursuit of justice and virtue, and that empty rhetoric, devoid of solid knowledge, is hollow and misleading. This leads us to consider the role of education in the formation of virtuous citizens and the pursuit of the common good.

As the dialogue progresses, Plato gifts us with an insightful analysis of human nature and the moral condition. Through the characters of Callicles and Polus, he exposes contrasting views on justice and desire. Callicles, representing the hedonistic current, argues that the pursuit of pleasure and power is the true basis of justice, while Polus, influenced by Socrates, defends the idea that true justice is intrinsically linked to reason and virtue. This dichotomy between hedonism and morality leads us to question the nature of our own desires and values, and how they shape our decisions and actions.

Moreover, *Gorgias* is not only a dialogue about rhetoric and justice but also about philosophy itself. Through Socrates' words, Plato leads us to reflect on the role of the philosopher in society. Socrates asserts that the true mission of the philosopher is to seek wisdom and truth, regardless of social conventions and empty rhetoric. He argues that the philosopher is someone who is dedicated to contemplation and the pursuit of knowledge, in contrast to the rhetorician who seeks only to persuade and impress. This view of the philosopher as a guardian of truth and virtue resonates deeply in the work and invites us to reflect on the role of philosophy in our own society.

The richness of the *Gorgias* dialogue also lies in how Plato uses irony and the Socratic method to guide the discussion. Socrates does not impose his ideas but draws them out through insightful questioning. This leads us to think for ourselves, to question our own beliefs, and to actively seek the truth. Through the Socratic method, Plato challenges us to be critical thinkers and not to blindly accept preconceived ideas.

Amidst the profusion of ideas and arguments presented in *Gorgias*, emerges a vital discussion about the interconnection between rhetoric and politics. Plato, through his characters, makes us question the influence of rhetoric in the public sphere. Through his critiques of empty rhetoric, he warns against speeches that aim solely at power and persuasion, neglecting the search for truth and justice. This reflection echoes in our modern times, as we are flooded by political and advertising discourses that often prioritize emotional appeal over substance and veracity. The work urges us to consider the responsibility of leaders and citizens in promoting a more ethical and informed rhetoric.

The interdisciplinarity of *Gorgias* is also a fascinating feature. The work is not limited to purely philosophical issues but also addresses themes that resonate in fields such as psychology, communication, politics, and ethics. The discussions on persuasion, knowledge, and morality are relevant not only in philosophy but in almost every aspect of our daily lives. Plato's work transcends the barriers of time and space, becoming an inexhaustible source of wisdom and reflection.

In summary, *Gorgias* is a profoundly captivating work that invites us to question and explore the nature of rhetoric, morality, and justice. Through intelligent dialogues and convincing arguments, Plato leads us on an intellectual journey that urges us to reflect on the importance of the search for truth, virtue, and justice in our daily lives. It is essential reading for anyone interested in philosophy and the pursuit of knowledge and wisdom, and it continues to resonate with its timeless relevance.

3rd Tetralogy

Meno

"Meno," one of the philosophical works in Plato's third tetralogy, is a dialogue that leads us into a profound reflection on knowledge, virtue, and the nature of learning. In this intriguing dialogue, Plato presents us with a riddle, a question that remains unsettling and relevant through the centuries: how can we acquire knowledge? Through a deep and meticulous analysis, Plato guides us through an intellectual labyrinth, shedding light on the principles of learning and the pursuit of virtue.

At the beginning of the dialogue, we encounter Meno, a young nobleman who questions Socrates about whether virtue can be taught. From this point, Plato takes us on a dialectical exploration that not only answers Meno's question but also leads us to consider fundamental issues about the nature of knowledge. The dialogue invites us to reflect on the relationship between pre-existing knowledge and learning, shedding light on Plato's theory of recollection.

One of the most striking features of "Meno" is the way Plato uses Socratic irony to guide the reader through a process of investigation and self-examination. Socrates, the main character in the dialogue, acts as an intellectual master of ceremonies, leading Meno and the reader to question their own beliefs and assumptions. Through a series of insightful questions and paradoxes, Socrates forces us to confront our own cognitive limitations and recognize the depth of our ignorance.

Furthermore, "Meno" presents a unique view of the Socratic method of questioning and dialogue. Plato shows us how Socrates not only seeks answers to specific questions but also promotes the process of self-knowledge and self-reflection. He invites us to explore the terrain of knowledge actively, to question our deeply held beliefs, and to seek truth in an inquisitive manner.

Plato's approach in "Meno" also highlights the importance of virtue in the pursuit of knowledge. He argues that virtue is intrinsically linked to wisdom, and that a virtuous individual is naturally inclined to seek knowledge and act according to high moral principles. The discussion about virtue and its relationship to knowledge raises profound questions about the nature of ethics and education, making "Meno" a fundamental text in moral philosophy.

Plato's unique approach in "Meno," within the third tetralogy, not only focuses on the pursuit of knowledge and virtue but also introduces the intriguing theory of recollection. This theory suggests that in our search for knowledge, we are not actually acquiring new information but rather recalling knowledge we already possess at some level. This idea challenges the conventional notion of learning and provides a surprising perspective on the nature of wisdom.

The theory of recollection presented by Plato in "Meno" is a fascinating idea that continues to intrigue philosophers and scholars to this day. It leads us to question the origin of knowledge and the nature of our mind. Do we truly possess innate knowledge that is simply waiting to be reactivated through reflection and investigation? Or is learning purely a process of accumulating external information? The theory of recollection opens a door to explore the complex relationship between the human mind and reality, challenging our traditional notions of learning.

Another captivating aspect of "Meno" is the way Plato explores the moral implications of the search for knowledge. He argues that virtue is closely tied to wisdom, and that a virtuous person is naturally inclined to seek knowledge and act according to high ethical principles. This viewpoint sheds light on the importance of ethical education and moral development in shaping a well-rounded individual. The discussion of virtue in "Meno" not only challenges us to reflect on what it means to be virtuous but also leads us to consider how education can shape human character and conduct.

Additionally, "Meno" serves as a testament to the Socratic method of questioning and dialogue. Socrates, with his interrogative approach, not only seeks answers to specific questions but also promotes the process of self-knowledge and self-reflection. By guiding Meno and other characters through a labyrinth of questions and paradoxes, Socrates forces them to confront their own cognitive limitations and recognize the depth of their ignorance. Through a constant process of self-examination, Plato shows us how the pursuit of knowledge is not only an intellectual journey but also a personal quest for self-understanding.

The intrinsic beauty of "Meno" lies in the way Plato weaves such a complex philosophical narrative with simplicity and clarity, making abstract and obscure questions accessible to any curious reader. The dialogue is like an intellectual puzzle, where the pieces fit skillfully, gradually revealing a broader and deeper picture. As we follow the discussion between Socrates and Meno, we are led to examine our own journey of discovering knowledge, inviting us to actively engage in the process of seeking truth.

The central question of the dialogue, whether virtue can be taught, is one that transcends time and culture, as it forces us to consider the nature of morality and ethics. The pursuit of virtue is a universal goal, and the discussion in "Meno" leads us to reflect on the role of education and self-improvement in shaping virtuous citizens. Plato's philosophical lessons, presented so engagingly, prompt us to consider how we can achieve a state of personal and collective virtue. The theory of recollection introduced by Plato also sheds intriguing light on the problem of knowledge. The idea that truth is something we already possess at some level, waiting to be rediscovered, is a thought-provoking perspective that challenges us to explore the mysteries of the human mind. This leads us to question our own innate ability to understand the world and invites us to consider whether knowledge is an external pursuit or an internal one.

Still, "Meno" is not just an abstract philosophical treatise; it is a lively and pulsating conversation between characters with distinct motivations and personalities. The interaction between Socrates, Meno, and other secondary characters is a key part of the dialogue's charm. As Socrates leads Meno on an unrelenting search for truth, we see the development of the characters and the transformations that occur in their perspectives. This human dimension adds depth to the work, making it not only an exploration of ideas but also a study of human nature.

In conclusion, Plato's "Meno" in the third tetralogy is a philosophical work that continues to astonish and challenge those who explore it. With its masterful approach, Plato takes us on a deep dive into the murky waters of knowledge, virtue, and learning. Through the engaging dialogue and Socratic method of questioning, he invites us to embark on a journey of self-knowledge and reflection. This work is a testament to humanity's eternal quest for wisdom and morality, and its impact resonates across the centuries, inspiring thinkers to dive into the unexplored ocean of philosophy in search of truth and excellence. "Meno" is not just a book, but a captivating intellectual experience that leads us to reflect on the deepest and most universal questions of human existence.

Euthyphro

"Euthyphro," one of Plato's most notable works, part of the third tetralogy, is a philosophical dialogue that delves into the complexities of morality, piety, and the nature of justice. Written around 399 BCE, this text invites us to reflect deeply on fundamental ethical questions, presenting a vivid portrayal of Socratic thought and the moral concerns of Ancient Greece. Through a series of dialogues between the philosopher Socrates and Euthyphro, an Athenian priest, Plato guides us through an intellectual maze that continues to challenge and inspire philosophers, scholars, and thinkers to this day.

At the heart of this dialogue lies the question that gives the work its title: "What is piety?" This seemingly simple dilemma opens the doors to a profound analysis of conceptions of morality, divinity, and justice in Greek society at the time. Socrates, known for his ability to question concepts taken as obvious, challenges Euthyphro to provide a satisfactory definition of piety. Through this challenge, Plato leads us on a philosophical journey full of twists and surprises.

One of the most captivating aspects of "Euthyphro" is the way Plato explores the relationship between morality and religion. Euthyphro, the priest, believes that piety is intrinsically linked to obedience to the gods and the performance of religious rituals. However, Socrates questions this view, suggesting that piety should be a universal virtue, independent of specific religious beliefs. This discussion raises fascinating questions about the nature of morality and how it is related to divinity, a theme that continues to resonate in contemporary moral philosophy.

As the dialogue progresses, Plato takes us on an intellectual journey that challenges us to think critically about what is right and wrong, and whether morality can be defined objectively or is relative to culture and individual belief. Socrates' arguments, often presented in the form of carefully crafted questions, invite us to examine our own beliefs and conceptions of virtue. This ability of Socrates to make his interlocutors reveal contradictions in their own arguments is one of the trademarks of the Socratic method and is in full force in "Euthyphro."

Another notable aspect of this dialogue is the complexity of the character of Euthyphro. He begins the conversation confident in his understanding of piety, but throughout the dialogue, his certainty is shaken by Socrates' incisive questions. This reflects Plato's skill in creating three-dimensional characters that evolve throughout the narrative, making the dialogue even more engaging and intriguing. However, like any great philosophical work, "Euthyphro" also leaves room for diverse interpretations. Scholars continue to debate to this day Plato's true intent in writing this dialogue. Some argue that he was seeking to challenge conventional understandings of piety and morality, while others believe that he was actually defending the importance of religion as the foundation of morality. This subtle ambiguity is part of what makes "Euthyphro" such a rich and thought-provoking work.

In addition to the ethical and religious questions that dominate the core of "Euthyphro," this work by Plato also offers a fascinating glimpse into Socrates' own personality. The philosopher is portrayed as an unrelenting questioner, someone who refuses to accept superficial definitions of moral and religious concepts. His approach, often ironic and challenging, incites those he dialogues with to think more deeply and re-examine their own premises. This leads us to reflect on the nature of Socratic philosophy as a constant effort to explore truth and wisdom through dialogue and inquiry.

Another intriguing aspect of "Euthyphro" is the role of knowledge and wisdom in morality. Socrates argues that true piety must be grounded in knowledge, not in mere blind obedience to the gods. He seeks to demonstrate that virtue and morality derive from correct understanding, which resonates with the famous Socratic maxim "Know thyself." This approach challenges the idea that morality is purely prescriptive and invites us to consider the importance of critical reflection and autonomous thinking in our moral actions.

The work also introduces us to the notion of moral dilemma, as Euthyphro faces the conflict between obeying a divine command he considers morally questionable and taking an action that seems more just. This raises universal questions about the clash between religious obedience and individual moral sense, a dilemma that remains relevant in our current society, where religious and ethical values often come into conflict.

However, it is important to recognize that "Euthyphro" leaves many questions unanswered. The precise definition of piety is never truly provided, and the dialogue ends ambiguously. Some may consider this a weakness, but others argue that this ambiguity is an essential part of the philosophical process, encouraging readers to continue the pursuit of knowledge and understanding.

"Euthyphro," this work by Plato that echoes through the centuries, retains its power to captivate the minds and hearts of contemporary readers and philosophers. One reason for its timelessness is Plato's ability to create dialogues that address issues that transcend the culture and era in which they were written. The search for the definition of piety and the interaction between morality and religion are themes that continue to challenge our understanding of the world, regardless of our cultural or religious tradition. The richness of "Euthyphro" also lies in its ability to raise important questions about the nature of truth. After all, Socrates, the great questioner, teaches us that the pursuit of truth involves not only seeking definitive answers but also being willing to constantly question, revise, and refine our ideas. This approach is a valuable reminder that philosophy should not be seen as a path to easy answers but as an ongoing process of investigation and self-discovery.

The ambiguity that permeates "Euthyphro" is another characteristic that makes it a standout philosophical work. Plato does not offer us a definitive solution to the dilemma of piety, leaving us with the task of continuing reflection and discussion. This reflects the complex and multifaceted nature of morality, which cannot be reduced to simplistic formulas. The ambiguity, far from being a weakness, is a strength, as it forces us to think deeply and embrace the uncertainty inherent in ethics.

Moreover, "Euthyphro" challenges us to consider the relationship between reason and faith. Although Plato is often associated with valuing reason, he does not ignore the spiritual dimension of human life. The dialogue reminds us that morality and religion can coexist in a complex and often conflicting manner, but they can also complement each other in ways that enrich our understanding of the world and our place in it.

"Euthyphro" is undoubtedly a gem of philosophy that, like a rare jewel, shines most brightly when exposed to the light of constant questioning. As the dialogue unfolds, we are confronted with the idea that piety cannot be reduced to a mere set of rules, but instead is a continuous pursuit of moral excellence. It makes us question our own understanding of morality and religion, forcing us to dive into the depths of our convictions and examine our own fallibilities.

A notable aspect of the work is how Socrates remains true to his commitment to lead intellectual inquiry without clinging to a preconceived position. By refusing to accept simplistic definitions of piety, he shows us the importance of intellectual humility and the willingness to recognize our own limitations. After all, the search for truth requires the ability to accept that we do not always have all the answers.

Furthermore, "Euthyphro" makes us reflect on the relationship between knowledge and virtue. The Socratic view that correct knowledge is intrinsically linked to morality is a powerful idea that continues to resonate in contemporary philosophy and ethics. This challenges us to seek a deeper understanding of the world and apply that knowledge virtuously in our lives.

Plato's ability to create complex characters, like Socrates and Euthyphro, is remarkable. Euthyphro, initially confident in his understanding of piety, is confronted with incisive questions that shake his certainty. This makes us reflect on the nature of wisdom and self-awareness as Euthyphro is led to deeply question his own beliefs. This aspect of the dialogue is a lesson on the importance of self-reflection and self-questioning in our pursuit of a virtuous life.

"Euthyphro" is therefore much more than just an ancient philosophical dialogue; it is an intellectual journey that continues to inspire and challenge generations of thinkers. Its ability to explore deep and universal questions of morality, religion, and knowledge makes it an essential work in the Western philosophical tradition. Plato invites us to enter a world of critical thinking and constant questioning, a world that encourages us to embrace uncertainty and pursue truth with passion and diligence. Thus, "Euthyphro" remains a beacon that illuminates the path of humanity's search for a deeper understanding of morality and virtue.

The Apology of Socrates

"The Apology of Socrates," written by Plato, stands out as a beacon in the vastness of classical philosophy. Belonging to the third tetralogy, this work plays a crucial role in the journey of the philosopher Socrates, one of the most influential figures in the history of philosophy. In this critical analysis, we will explore the depth and relevance of this unique work, highlighting its qualities and contextualizing its significance.

The plot unfolds like a philosophical drama, in which Socrates faces accusations of corrupting the youth and introducing new deities. Through a passionate and persuasive speech, the philosopher defends his cause before an Athenian court, demonstrating intellectual courage that echoes through the centuries. In Plato's words, Socrates' brilliant mind and his unique approach to philosophy are revealed. What makes "The Apology of Socrates" truly captivating is the depiction of Socrates as a man of unwavering principles, refusing to compromise his pursuit of truth, even in the face of the prospect of his own death sentence. Socrates, as portrayed by Plato, emerges as a timeless example of intellectual integrity and moral resilience, inspiring all those dedicated to the pursuit of knowledge and wisdom.

The dialogue between Socrates and his accusers reveals a spectacle of rhetorical skill and philosophical argumentation. Socrates skillfully challenges his opponents, exposing the fragility of their accusations and leading them to question their own beliefs. This ability of Socrates to question established notions and reveal the underlying ignorance is a valuable lesson that transcends antiquity and remains relevant to this day. Furthermore, "The Apology of Socrates" offers a fascinating glimpse into Athenian society of the time. The work depicts the values, prejudices, and the justice system of classical Athens, providing important historical context for understanding the interactions between Socrates and his contemporaries. The narrative also highlights the tension between philosophy and established authority, a recurring theme in the history of philosophy.

Throughout "The Apology of Socrates," Plato reminds us of the importance of the pursuit of truth, intellectual integrity, and constant questioning. The work serves as an eternal tribute to Socrates' legacy and his unwavering commitment to philosophy. His teachings continue to inspire generations of thinkers, reminding us that philosophy, above all, is an act of courage and dedication to the relentless search for knowledge. Through the words meticulously recorded by Plato, we are invited to witness the process by which Socrates conducts his own trial. He argues that he has no declared enemies, that he does not profess strange cults, and in doing so, he urges us to reflect on the nature of the accusation against him. It is an accusation that goes beyond mere allegations of crimes. It is an accusation against the very essence of Socratic philosophy, which, in turn, is a critique of the core of Athenian society at the time. Through this insightful dialogue, Plato reminds us that the confrontation between philosophy and the polis is a recurring and timeless theme, where inconvenient truths are often rejected in favor of established conventions.

One of the most notable characteristics of "The Apology of Socrates" is Socrates' attitude toward his own imminent death. Instead of demonstrating fear or despair, Socrates faces his death sentence with a serenity and resignation that defy conventional understanding of death. He argues that death is unknown, and the unknown is precisely what philosophy strives to comprehend. Socrates, thus, transforms his own death into a philosophical act, an act of the search for knowledge, a testimony that philosophy is not a mere intellectual exercise, but a way of living and dying with dignity.

The lasting impact of "The Apology of Socrates" extends beyond the Athenian court. It is a work that resonates in all times, reminding us of the importance of freedom of thought, the ability to question, and the unwavering commitment to the pursuit of truth. Through the words of Socrates and the pen of Plato, we are challenged to question our own convictions, to confront established authority, and to never cease exploring the depths of philosophy.

The influence of Plato's "The Apology of Socrates" cannot be overstated, as it transcends time and space, continuing to be a source of inspiration and challenge for philosophers, scholars, and seekers of truth. Socrates, through his passionate defense, teaches us that philosophy is not a mere intellectual abstraction, but a discipline that is directly related to human life and its most fundamental issues. He embodies the relentless search for wisdom, regardless of adversity, and reminds us that true wisdom lies in the awareness of our own ignorance. Socrates' approach in "The Apology" also challenges the traditional division between ethics and epistemology. Through his relentless questions and dialogues with the

Athenians, he not only seeks the truth but also promotes self-reflection and personal responsibility. Socrates argues that virtue is intrinsically linked to knowledge, that acting rightly is the result of understanding what is right. This view is a tribute to the importance of cultivating one's own mind and the fundamental role of education in the formation of virtuous citizens.

Another notable aspect of "The Apology of Socrates" is the Socratic irony, a rhetorical technique by which Socrates feigns ignorance to expose the ignorance of his interlocutors. This serves not only as a tool to enhance the argument but also as a constant reminder that intellectual humility and the willingness to admit our own ignorance are fundamental virtues in the pursuit of knowledge.

Plato's "The Apology of Socrates," in the third tetralogy, is a remarkable testament to Socrates' intellectual courage and the depth of the philosophy he practiced. In this moving dialogue, we see a man who chose to face the prospect of death with dignity rather than renounce his philosophical principles. Socrates reminds us that true philosophy is much more than a mere academic exercise; it is a way of living and dying, a pursuit that transcends the simple accumulation of knowledge. Socrates' eloquent defense before his trial is a timeless lesson in rhetoric and argumentation. Socrates' skill in deconstructing the accusations of his opponents and revealing the weakness of their arguments is a brilliant example of how philosophy can be applied in the real world. He not only contests the allegations against him but also exposes the need to question our own beliefs and prejudices.

The central issue of "The Apology" is the relationship between philosophy and society. Socrates, as a philosopher, represents the figure who challenges the status quo and asks uncomfortable questions. He questions traditional beliefs, challenges conventions, and urges his contemporaries to examine their lives and their deeper convictions. The work reminds us that philosophy has the power to disrupt established structures and incite change, often facing considerable resistance. Furthermore, "The Apology of Socrates" emphasizes the importance of freedom of thought and expression. Socrates' ability to articulate his ideas and defend his actions before a court that was willing to condemn him to death is a testament to the need to protect the space for critical thinking and dissent in any society. The work continues to remind us that intellectual freedom is a precious achievement that must be preserved and nurtured.

Ultimately, "The Apology of Socrates" is a tribute to the transformative power of philosophy and the courage required to face the consequences of challenging social and political conventions. Socrates, as portrayed by Plato, remains a beacon of wisdom, inspiring us never to stop questioning, to embrace the search for truth, and to defend our convictions, even in the face of adversity. This work is a lesson for all ages, reminding us that philosophy is more than words; it is a force that can change the world and challenge us to seek a deeper and more meaningful understanding of human existence.

Crito

"Crito," the second dialogue of Plato's third tetralogy, is a work that stands out not only for the richness of its philosophical discussions but also for the depth of its moral and ethical reflections. In this dialogue, Plato presents an aging Socrates, about to face his death sentence imposed by the city of Athens. Through an engaging and insightful dialogue with his friend Crito, Plato leads us to question the nature of justice, obedience to the law, and morality, offering a penetrating view of the conflicts between loyalty to the state and moral duty.

The first notable feature of this dialogue is Plato's ability to create an atmosphere of urgency and tension, which draws us in from the beginning. Crito, worried about Socrates' impending execution, tries to persuade him to escape from prison and avoid his condemnation. However, Socrates refuses to give in to his pleas, arguing that justice is an unbreakable principle that cannot be subverted, even in the face of death. This moral conflict is the heart of the dialogue and serves as a starting point for a series of profound discussions about the nature of justice and obedience to the law.

One of the central issues addressed in "Crito" is the relationship between the individual and the state. Socrates argues that obedience to the law is a moral duty that all citizens must follow, even when they disagree with the decisions of the city. He defends the idea that the city, as a wise and just entity, should be obeyed as one would obey a father or guardian. This view places the authority of the state above personal opinions and establishes a high ethical standard for citizens' conduct.

However, Crito presents persuasive arguments in favor of Socrates' escape. He claims that Socrates' death will be an irreparable loss to philosophy and the community, and that the escape would be justified to preserve his legacy. This tension between the moral duty to obey the law and the desire to preserve the common good creates a captivating ethical dilemma that challenges the reader to reflect on the limits of civil disobedience and the universal principles of justice. Furthermore, "Crito" offers a fascinating insight into Socrates' personality and his steadfast character. By refusing to escape, Socrates demonstrates his unwavering dedication to truth and philosophy, even in the face of death. His attitude challenges the reader to consider how far they are willing to go in defense of their convictions, reinforcing the notion that truth and virtue are supreme values that must be preserved at all costs.

In "Crito," Plato invites us to explore the conflict between obedience to the law and individual morality in a captivating and profound way. Through a series of meticulously constructed arguments, he presents us with a moral dilemma that is timeless and universal. The question that looms over the dialogue is: to what extent are we willing to sacrifice our own life in the name of justice and moral integrity? Socrates' response is clear and uncompromising: justice cannot be subordinated to personal interests or the pressure of public opinion. This challenges us to rethink our own priorities and examine whether we are capable of upholding our ethical principles, even when confronted with consequences as grave as death.

Another notable aspect of "Crito" is how Plato uses the dialogue to explore the relationship between knowledge and virtue. Socrates argues that acting unjustly is, ultimately, the result of ignorance, since no one would consciously act wrong. Therefore, he emphasizes the importance of knowledge in the pursuit of virtue and justice. This connection between wisdom and virtue resonates throughout all of Plato's work and remains a central theme in moral philosophy.

Moreover, "Crito" provides us with a fascinating view of philosophy as a transformative force in Socrates' life. Through his commitment to the pursuit of truth and virtue, Socrates shows that philosophy is not just an intellectual exercise, but also a way of life that can lead us to question our own convictions and improve our conduct. Socrates, the philosopher, becomes an inspiring example of moral integrity and intellectual courage, and his stance before death is the personification of philosophy as a path to wisdom and self-realization.

At the heart of the "Crito" dialogue lies the intricate idea that justice is not merely a social convention, but a deep moral imperative that transcends the world of human laws. Through the figure of Socrates, Plato reminds us that justice is an inherent force in human nature, a quality that resides at the core of each individual and must be preserved at all costs. This leads us to reflect on the relationship between personal morality and the laws of society, challenging us to question whether obeying unjust laws is truly a virtuous act, or if, in some cases, disobedience may be the most courageous and just attitude.

In response to Crito's persuasion, Socrates argues that one should not fear death, as the uncertainty surrounding it makes it impossible to know whether it is a blessing or a curse. He reminds us that true wisdom lies in recognizing ignorance, and this intellectual humility allows us to face death with serenity. This view of death as a passage into the unknown, rather than an event to be feared, is one of Plato's enduring contributions to philosophy and the way it shapes our understanding of life and death.

Another captivating element of "Crito" is the complexity of the friendship between Socrates and Crito. Although Crito is determined to save his friend's life, Socrates refuses to allow their friendship to cloud his moral judgment. His devotion to justice is so unwavering that he rejects the escape, even when Crito offers him the opportunity to flee. This dynamic makes us question the nature of true friendship and how far we should be willing to go against our friends' wishes in the name of moral righteousness.

"Crito" transcends the barriers of time and culture to continue inspiring and intriguing, leaving us immersed in a sea of philosophical questioning about the nature of duty, morality, and justice. Plato uses the mastery of dialogue to delve deeply into the minds of the characters, forcing us to think critically about the moral decisions that confront Socrates and Crito. In this sense, "Crito" serves as an eternal lesson for humanity, reminding us of the need to maintain moral integrity regardless of adverse circumstances.

The dialogue also sheds light on the relationship between the individual and society. The city of Athens, represented by the law that sentenced Socrates to death, is portrayed as a paternal figure whose authority and wisdom must be respected. However, Crito questions whether the city is acting justly in condemning Socrates, and whether respect for the law is always the right path to follow. This conflict between respect for authority and the pursuit of personal justice is a perpetual dichotomy that continues to resonate in our society, as we question when we should defy established laws in the name of justice and morality.

Throughout the dialogue, Socrates reminds us that truth and virtue are intrinsically linked. He argues that acting unjustly is the result of ignorance, as no one would deliberately do wrong. This encourages us to seek knowledge and wisdom as the key to achieving virtue and living a just life. Socrates' approach to philosophy as a means of self-reflection and moral improvement resonates deeply in our understanding of philosophy as a quest for wisdom and truth.

Furthermore, the figure of Socrates in "Crito" embodies intellectual courage and steadfast character. He refuses to escape from prison, even when faced with the prospect of death, demonstrating that the pursuit of truth and adherence to ethical principles are non-negotiable. Socrates' courage is a timeless reminder that moral integrity is an ideal that must be pursued, regardless of personal consequences.

In summary, "Crito" is a deeply relevant and timeless philosophical work that invites us to delve into the complexities of morality, justice, and obedience to the law. With its captivating prose and insightful arguments, Plato challenges us to reflect on our own values and examine how far we are willing to go in the name of justice and virtue. This dialogue continues to be a beacon of wisdom and an inexhaustible source of moral reflection, providing lessons that resonate through eternity and shape our understanding of the complexities of ethics and philosophy. "Crito" remains a lasting testament to the tireless pursuit of truth and justice, a constant reminder that moral and ethical questions remain fundamental in our journey as human beings.

4th Tetralogy

The Symposium

Plato's "The Symposium" is a work that has endured through the centuries as a brilliant example of philosophy and classical literature. This work, part of Plato's 4th tetralogy of dialogues, is one of the jewels of ancient Greek philosophy and offers us a profound and comprehensive view of discussions about love, beauty, wisdom, and human nature.

The dialogue begins with a gathering of friends, including Socrates, who narrates the story. They meet at the house of the poet Agathon to celebrate his victory in a dramatic competition and, more importantly, to discuss the theme of love. The festive atmosphere and lively conversation provide the perfect backdrop for the deep reflections that unfold throughout the dialogue.

One of the captivating features of "The Symposium" is how Plato uses the dialogue as a vehicle for presenting various perspectives on love. Each character offers a different view on what love is, and Socrates acts as the master of ceremonies, guiding the discussion with his unparalleled philosophical skills. This creates a dynamic interaction between the characters that keeps the reader engaged and curious to discover the truth about love.

The depth of the ideas discussed in "The Symposium" is another reason why this work is so captivating. Plato explores the nature of love from various perspectives, from physical love to spiritual love, from the love between lovers to the love of wisdom. Through the words of his characters, Plato invites us to reflect on the true meaning of love and its connection to the pursuit of truth and beauty.

Additionally, the work is captivating for its connection to the theory of Forms, one of the central ideas in Platonic philosophy. Through the words of Diotima, a wise woman whom Socrates mentions, we are introduced to the idea that love is a quest for beauty and immortality. This leads us into a fascinating discussion about the nature of the Forms and how they relate to the sensible world.

The beauty of Plato's language and reasoning in "The Symposium" also deserves attention. His dialogues are written with precision and elegance that captivate the reader, making philosophy accessible and engaging. Every word is carefully chosen, and each argument is presented logically and convincingly. The beauty of "The Symposium" lies not only in the diversity of perspectives on love but also in how Plato unites them into a unified and profound vision. The dialogue leads us to understand that love is much more than simple physical or emotional attraction.

Through his words, Plato guides us to the understanding that love is a powerful force that drives us toward transcendence, the pursuit of absolute truth and beauty, which he conceives as the ideal Forms. The figure of Diotima, the wise woman whom Socrates mentions, is especially captivating in this context. She leads us through the stages of the "ladder of love," which culminates in the contemplation of the Forms, and ultimately, in the quest for supreme truth. This philosophical journey is captivating and inspiring, inviting the reader to reflect on the depths of love and its transformative potential.

Another notable aspect of "The Symposium" is how Plato uses the characters to represent different views and approaches to love. Agathon, the host of the party, extols love as a benevolent and divine force. On the other hand, Aristophanes presents a fun and imaginative theory that humans were originally spherical creatures, and love is the desire to reunite with one's "other half." These diverse perspectives not only make the work more captivating but also shed light on the complexity of love and human nature.

Moreover, Plato's ability to create engaging and profound dialogues is evident in "The Symposium." The characters are vivid, their personalities and voices distinct, and their discussions are filled with moments of insight and humor. Socrates, as the master of dialectic, leads the conversations masterfully, guiding the characters and the reader to delve deeper into philosophical issues.

We must not forget that "The Symposium" is a work that continues to echo in our culture, influencing the way we see love and philosophy to this day. The idea of love as a pursuit of truth and beauty transcends eras and continues to inspire thinkers, writers, and artists. Plato's dialogue transcends its time and becomes a perennial source of reflection and inspiration.

The captivation that "The Symposium" exerts on its readers goes beyond the words written by Plato, extending to its ability to provoke deep reflections and endless discussions. The questions raised in the dialogue about love, beauty, the nature of the soul, and the quest for truth transcend time and cultural barriers. It is remarkable how Plato manages to make us think about issues that are as relevant today as they were in ancient Athens.

In this context, the dialogue also reveals the inherently dialectical nature of philosophy. Ideas are presented, debated, and refined as the characters express their views and refute each other's arguments. This highlights the importance of dialogue and questioning as essential tools in the pursuit of truth. "The Symposium" is not just a philosophical text; it is a practical guide to how philosophy is done, with Socrates acting as a skilled guide on this journey of intellectual exploration.

The complexity of "The Symposium" is also a constant source of captivation. As the dialogue progresses, we are led to reflect on the connections between the different viewpoints presented and to question our own understanding of love and the pursuit of truth. The theory of Forms, with its distinction between the sensible world and the world of eternal ideas, further enriches the intellectual fabric, providing a deep metaphysical framework for the discussions.

At the heart of Plato's "The Symposium," part of the 4th tetralogy of dialogues, we find an incessant search for the essence of humanity. As Socrates guides his friends and the reader through the complex discussions on love and beauty, we are led to consider not only the abstract elements of philosophical discourse but also our own human experience. The work forces us to look into the mirror of our soul, to question our own desires, and to reflect on what we truly value in life.

One of the most emblematic passages of the dialogue occurs when Socrates recounts the teachings of Diotima on love as a journey of spiritual ascent. This narrative challenges us to transcend our most basic instincts and to seek a higher love that leads us toward wisdom and immortality. Beauty, in this context, ceases to be merely a physical characteristic and becomes a reflection of the harmony of the ideal Forms. It is as though Plato reminds us that the search for the beautiful and the true is a search for perfection, one that can elevate the human soul to a higher state of consciousness.

Another captivating aspect of "The Symposium" is the representation of human desire as a driving force. Aristophanes, with his theory of the separated halves, extols the idea that love is the desire to find our "other half," a deep longing that propels us to seek completeness. This view is deeply captivating because it resonates with the universal experience of desire and the search for connection.

Thus, Plato reminds us that love, in its many forms and manifestations, is an inextricable part of the human experience. The complexity of "The Symposium" is one of the reasons why the work continues to fascinate readers and scholars. The dialogues that unfold at Agathon's party, with their arguments and counterpoints, provide a vivid portrait of the Socratic method and the intricate nature of philosophical issues. Each character contributes unique perspectives and profound questioning, creating a mosaic of ideas that is captivating in its diversity and depth.

Ultimately, Plato's "The Symposium" transcends mere discussion of love and beauty. It is an invitation to a continuous exploration of the fundamental questions of human existence. As we dive into the pages of this dialogue, we are challenged to question, reflect, and become active participants in the pursuit of truth and wisdom. Captivating, profound, and eternally relevant, Plato's "The Symposium" continues to be a work that inspires us to explore the depths of the human condition and to engage in the tireless pursuit of understanding. It is an intellectual feast that satisfies our hunger for knowledge and, at the same time, leaves us with a voracious appetite for more.

Phaedrus

"Phaedrus," written by Plato in the 4th Tetralogy, is one of the most enigmatic and influential works in Western philosophy. In this dialogue, Plato presents us with a profound exploration of rhetoric, love, the soul, and writing, all intertwined in a captivating narrative that challenges the reader to reflect on fundamental questions of human existence.

One of the most striking characteristics of "Phaedrus" is its dialogue structure, where Socrates and Phaedrus discuss philosophical concepts while walking along the banks of the Ilisus River in Athens. This idyllic setting provides an impressive backdrop for the complex ideas Plato explores throughout the work. As the two characters converse, Plato leads us on a philosophical journey that moves from questions of rhetoric and persuasion to a deeper analysis of the role of love in human life.

Plato, through Socrates, argues that writing is an inferior form of communication compared to speech. He believes that writing is static and cannot adapt to the reader's needs, unlike speech, which allows for dynamic interaction. This critique of writing is one of the most intriguing parts of "Phaedrus," as it makes us question the nature of communication and the transmission of knowledge. It is a critique that remains relevant in our digital age, where written communication often feels cold and impersonal.

The dialogue between Socrates and Phaedrus also takes us into a deep analysis of love, which Plato describes as one of the most powerful forces of the human soul. He argues that love is what drives the pursuit of knowledge and wisdom, and that it is through love that souls can attain immortality. These reflections on love and immortality add a poetic and emotional dimension to "Phaedrus," making it a work that goes beyond mere rational analysis.

Furthermore, "Phaedrus" also addresses the issue of rhetoric and persuasion. Plato warns about the dangers of empty and manipulative rhetoric, which can be used to deceive people rather than lead them to knowledge and truth. This critique of superficial rhetoric is a timeless lesson, especially in a world where the manipulation of information is a constant concern. Additionally, Plato's "Phaedrus" in the 4th Tetralogy challenges conventional conceptions of speech and writing, opening doors for a deeper exploration of the philosophy of language. Through the character of Socrates, Plato argues that writing is unable to answer questions and objections in real time, while oral communication allows for a dynamic exchange of ideas. This leads us to reflect on how language shapes our thinking and our ability to explore complex concepts.

Another notable aspect of "Phaedrus" is the discussion of the importance of love and beauty in human life. Plato presents the idea that love is a force that compels us to seek beauty, and through this process, to attain wisdom. He invites us to consider how love shapes our actions and choices, leading us to question the nature and origin of this powerful motivating force. From the analysis of various forms of love, Plato also offers us an intriguing view of platonic love, which is based on the pursuit of truth and beauty in the souls of others. This concept of love transcends the physical aspect and suggests that true connection lies at the core of the soul, where the pursuit of knowledge and wisdom becomes the ultimate goal.

However, "Phaedrus" also warns us about the dangers of love when it is excessive and devoid of wisdom. Plato presents the myth of Eros, which cautions about the risk of being swept away by uncontrolled passions, which can lead to moral and spiritual degradation. This duality of love, as both a redemptive and destructive force, is a recurring theme in philosophy and literature, and Plato explores it masterfully in his work.

Nevertheless, we cannot overlook the complexity of Plato's writing in "Phaedrus," which often challenges interpretation. His prose is rich in metaphors and imagery, which can make the reading challenging for some. However, it is this richness and depth that makes "Phaedrus" such a captivating and enduring work. Each subsequent reading reveals new layers of meaning and insights, making it an inexhaustible source of philosophical reflection.

Through the character of Phaedrus, Plato also addresses the question of the reincarnation of the soul, a theme that adds depth to the discussion of the nature of the soul and its destiny. The idea that the soul may have existed in previous lives and that its journey is influenced by past relationships and loves sheds intriguing light on the understanding of the human being. This leads us to think about the continuity of the soul and the importance of interpersonal bonds in our spiritual journey.

Another captivating aspect of "Phaedrus" is the way in which Plato explores the nature of writing and orality in relation to philosophy and the transmission of knowledge. Plato's critique of writing, arguing that it is static and incapable of answering questions, leads us to consider the importance of philosophical dialogue, where the exchange of ideas and the confrontation of points of view can lead to a deeper understanding of truth. This critique of writing serves as a powerful reminder that philosophy is a living endeavor, one that must be discussed and debated, not just passively read.

Moreover, "Phaedrus" also invites us to reflect on the nature of rhetoric and persuasion. Plato, through Socrates, warns about the dangers of deceptive rhetoric, which can be used to manipulate and deceive people. This critique is relevant in our current society, where persuasion and the manipulation of information are powerful tools. "Phaedrus" reminds us of the importance of discerning truth from falsehood and seeking wisdom rather than being simply persuaded by eloquent but empty arguments.

In his masterful dialogue, Plato also presents us with an intriguing myth, the myth of Thammuz, which addresses the cyclical nature of time and the rebirth of the soul. This myth, with its deep roots in Greek mythology, adds a layer of symbolism to the work and invites us to contemplate the eternity of the soul, which transcends the limitations of earthly life. Through this myth, Plato transports us to a philosophical dimension where time and space dissolve, leaving only the essence of the soul as a beacon guiding our search for truth.

Furthermore, the discussion of the art of rhetoric in "Phaedrus" is a perennial lesson on the importance of ethics in communication. Socrates warns against the irresponsible use of rhetoric, emphasizing that empty persuasion, devoid of wisdom and truth, can be harmful to society. This message resonates strongly in our era of manipulative political speeches and false information, highlighting the need for an ethical approach to communication and persuasion.

Plato's eloquent writing in "Phaedrus" is also an example of the author's literary and philosophical mastery. His dialogues are like literary works of art that transport us to a world of ideas and deep reflections. His metaphors and poetic images beautify philosophical prose, making reading an aesthetic experience that enchants the reader and engages them in a unique way. However, we cannot ignore the complexity and ambiguity that permeate "Phaedrus." The work challenges the reader to explore the contradictions and paradoxes of Platonic philosophy, pushing us beyond easy answers and simplistic conclusions. It is a work that invites us to embrace ambiguity and uncertainty, to reflect on the complexities of human existence, and to embrace the ceaseless search for knowledge.

In "Phaedrus," Plato invites us to dive into the deep waters of philosophy and rhetoric, exploring the dynamic between oral speech and writing, love and the soul, and truth and persuasion. It is a work that challenges us to rethink the nature of communication and the importance of the pursuit of knowledge. In doing so, Plato pushes us beyond the limits of our conventional understanding and urges us to explore the most hidden corners of human experience. One of the most impressive features of "Phaedrus" is Plato's ability to blend poetry and philosophy. His metaphors and poetic images are like rays of light that illuminate the path of philosophical reflection. He invites us to contemplate the beauty of language and the depth of ideas, challenging us to look beyond the words to capture the essence of truth. This fusion of poetry and philosophy gives "Phaedrus" a uniqueness that makes it irresistible to those seeking an intellectual and aesthetic experience.

Ultimately, "Phaedrus" is a work that transcends time and culture, captivating readers from all eras. Its poetic prose, philosophical reflections, and its call to the pursuit of truth and wisdom continue to inspire those who seek to unravel the mysteries of human existence. It is a work that challenges us, enchants us, and impels us to explore the complexities of language, love, and the soul. It is an intellectual journey worth undertaking, time and time again, throughout our lives.

The Republic

"The Republic," a seminal work of philosophy written by Plato, one of the most influential thinkers of classical antiquity, is part of the fourth tetralogy of the author's works. This dialogue stands out for its depth and complexity, exploring themes ranging from justice and education to politics and the nature of the human soul. Through an engaging narrative, Plato leads us through a rich territory of ideas that challenge our understanding of the world and society. In this critical review, we will explore some of the most striking aspects of "The Republic" and how this work continues to inspire thinkers and philosophers over the centuries.

One of the most remarkable features of "The Republic" is the way Plato invites us to engage in a philosophical dialogue that takes place between Socrates and various other characters, such as Glaucon, Adeimantus, and Thrasymachus. This dialogical approach allows ideas to be debated and examined from multiple perspectives, creating a rich and stimulating intellectual environment. The reader is led to question their own beliefs and explore complex concepts, such as the nature of justice and the ideal society, in a way that transcends mere theoretical discourse.

The search for justice is one of the central themes of "The Republic." Plato argues that justice is more than mere convenience or obedience to established laws. He takes us on a philosophical journey that makes us question what is just and how a just society should be structured. By challenging conventional notions of justice, Plato forces us to reflect on the intrinsic nature of good and evil, and how these concepts relate to the organization of society and individual morality.

Another notable aspect of "The Republic" is the famous allegory of the cave, presented in Book VII. This allegory serves as a powerful metaphor for the pursuit of knowledge and truth. Plato describes a group of people who have spent their entire lives chained in a cave, looking at a wall where shadows are projected. These shadows represent the illusion of the sensible world, and Plato argues that true reality lies beyond these shadows, in the form of eternal ideas and concepts. The journey of leaving the cave and contemplating the sunlight symbolizes the pursuit of knowledge and truth, inviting us to question the nature of reality and perception.

Additionally, "The Republic" also addresses education and the formation of character, emphasizing the importance of cultivating virtue and wisdom. Plato argues that education should be directed toward the formation of guardians of the city, individuals who possess a deep sense of duty and justice. He proposes a rigorous curriculum that includes music, mathematics, and philosophy, in order to shape the minds and hearts of future leaders of society. However, "The Republic" is not only a work that provides definitive answers, but one that stimulates critical thinking and constant questioning. The ambiguity present in many of Plato's dialogues reminds us of the complexity of the search for knowledge and the difficulty of reaching absolute conclusions.

Plato's "The Republic" transcends the barrier of time, continuing to resonate in our contemporary world, provoking deep debates about the nature of justice and society. Plato's ability to question conventions and challenge our preconceived notions is one of the reasons why this work remains so fascinating and relevant.

Plato's vision of the ideal society, presented in Book V of "The Republic," is one of the highlights of the work. He proposes a city where justice reigns supreme, where the division of classes is based on each individual's aptitude and vocation, and where property is shared. This philosophical utopia, although often considered impractical, challenges us to think about alternatives to our current social and economic system.

Plato's concern with education extends beyond the formation of just leaders; it also encompasses the creation of a culture that promotes virtue and wisdom. Music and poetry are seen as powerful influences on the mind and morals of people, and Plato proposes a strict censorship to ensure that only art that promotes desired values is allowed. This leads us to question the delicate balance between freedom of expression and the need to guide culture toward ethical goals.

Furthermore, the allegory of the cave, mentioned earlier, not only represents a quest for knowledge but also offers a deep insight into the nature of perception and reality. Plato argues that the sensible world we perceive through our senses is merely a shadow of the true reality of eternal ideas. This metaphor challenges us to question our understanding of reality and the importance of the search for truth in a world permeated by illusions and deceptive appearances.

"The Republic" is a work that requires time and reflection to be truly appreciated. The wealth of ideas and concepts that Plato presents is an invitation to deep exploration and ongoing intellectual debate. His writing style, through dialogues between characters, is engaging and captivating, providing the reader with a sense of active participation in the philosophical discussions.

The influence of Plato's "The Republic" on philosophy, politics, and education over the centuries is undeniable. His ideas continue to be debated, reinterpreted, and applied in various contexts. Plato's view of philosophy as a means to attain wisdom and guide society serves as a constant reminder of the importance of intellectual reflection in our lives. The dialogue between Socrates and his interlocutors is not only a vehicle for Plato's ideas but also an example of how philosophy should be practiced. The Socratic approach, based on relentless questioning and the search for truth, is a valuable lesson for all aspiring thinkers.

Plato reminds us that truth is not something that can simply be transmitted passively but must be discovered through dialogue and constant questioning. Furthermore, Plato's analysis of the nature of the human soul is profoundly insightful. He describes the soul as composed of three parts: reason, spirit, and appetite. This internal division helps us better understand our motivations and the constant struggle between the desire for immediate pleasure and the pursuit of higher values. Reflecting on the nature of the soul invites us to explore our own motivations and seek inner harmony.

The legacy of "The Republic" also extends to politics and the theory of the state. The notion that justice should be the fundamental principle of any society is an ideal embraced by many philosophers and politicians throughout history. Plato's search for a just and well-ordered city, where each citizen plays a role according to their abilities and vocations, continues to inspire utopian visions and discussions about the role of government and justice in society.

Plato's "The Republic," part of the fourth tetralogy of his works, transcends time and history, standing as a beacon of philosophical thought that continues to illuminate our intellectual and moral paths. Plato's ability to delve into the depths of human nature, justice, politics, and education is remarkable, and his approach through captivating dialogues sets a standard of intellectual engagement that resonates to this day. By entering the intricacies of Plato's discussions, we are immersed in a world of idea exchange that challenges our beliefs and preconceived concepts. The Socratic dialectic, with Socrates acting as the master of incisive questioning, leads us to an incessant exploration of the notions of justice and virtue. The dialogue calls us to transcend the superficiality of common opinions and dig deep into the quest for true understanding, highlighting the importance of critical reflection in our own lives.

Plato's vision of the ideal society, outlined in Book V of "The Republic," is an audacious proposal that challenges the status quo. He invites us to consider a city where justice reigns supreme, where classes are defined based on individual skills and vocations, and where property is shared. While this utopia is often seen as impractical, it continues to stimulate debates about the structure of our own society and economy, raising pertinent questions about equality and fairness.

Education, under Plato's keen scrutiny, is not limited to the acquisition of knowledge but also involves the formation of character and morality. His proposal for a rigorous curriculum, encompassing music, mathematics, and philosophy, emphasizes the importance of culture in shaping individuals and society as a whole. Plato's reflections on censorship in art and poetry, to ensure that only those works promoting desired values are allowed, urge us to question the delicate balance between freedom of expression and the ethical guidance of culture.

The allegory of the cave, in Book VII, represents a powerful metaphor that transcends the ages. It challenges the way we perceive reality, pointing out that the sensible world, which we experience through our senses, is only a shadow of the true reality that resides in eternal ideas. This allegory leads us to question not only the nature of reality but also the importance of the relentless search for truth in a world often obscured by illusions and prejudices.

Moreover, Plato's analysis of the human soul, divided into three parts: reason, spirit, and appetite, provides a profound understanding of the complexity of human nature. This internal division helps us decipher our motivations and internal conflicts, a valuable lesson for self-knowledge and self-transformation. The struggles between the desire for immediate pleasure and the pursuit of higher values resonate in our own experiences, inviting us to reflect on our choices and aspirations.

In summary, Plato's "The Republic" is a monument of philosophy that continues to captivate and inspire us. Its exploration of justice, education, the nature of the soul, and politics is a deep and timeless intellectual journey. This work reminds us that philosophy is not merely the search for definitive answers but an ongoing journey of questioning, reflection, and self-discovery. As we contemplate Plato's teachings, we are reminded that the pursuit of knowledge and wisdom is an endless journey, and that philosophy, with its perpetual questions, remains a reliable compass in our efforts to understand the world and ourselves.

Phaedo

"Phaedo," one of the most profound and philosophically rich works of Plato's fourth tetralogy, captivates the reader from the very first paragraph, taking them on an intellectual journey of reflection and inquiry that resonates through the centuries. In this dialogue, Plato presents Socrates on the day of his execution, a moment of profound transition in his life and in the history of philosophy. Through insightful dialogues and convincing arguments, Plato explores crucial themes such as the immortality of the soul, the nature of death, and the value of philosophy as preparation for life after death.

In an era of quick answers and superficiality, *Phaedo* invites us to dive into the complexities of philosophical thought. Plato, using Socrates as his spokesperson, challenges conventional notions about death, asserting that true philosophy is a training for death. The dialogue exposes the belief that the soul is immortal and that the pursuit of knowledge and virtue is the essential preparation for the afterlife. Through solid arguments, Plato constructs a meticulous defense of this perspective, shaking our conventional beliefs about mortality and encouraging us to think more deeply about the meaning of human existence.

The brilliance of *Phaedo* lies in Plato's ability to fuse emotional and rational elements into a cohesive narrative. By presenting Socrates on his deathbed, surrounded by his disciples, he creates an atmosphere of intense emotion and sympathy, allowing us to identify with Socrates' pain and farewell. At the same time, the sharp logic of Socrates' arguments challenges us to reconsider our own beliefs about mortality, forcing us to contemplate the implications of our actions and choices in life.

Another remarkable aspect of *Phaedo* is Plato's mastery in constructing complex arguments in an accessible way. He uses ingenious metaphors and analogies, such as the lyre and its tuning, to explain abstract concepts in a tangible manner. This makes philosophy more palatable and invites the reader to actively engage in the discussion. As the characters debate the nature of the soul, the relationship between body and mind, and the validity of philosophy as preparation for death, we are challenged to think deeply and question our own assumptions.

However, *Phaedo* is not just an abstract exploration of philosophical concepts; it is a reflection on life itself and the quest for knowledge. Socrates, with his serenity in the face of imminent death, personifies the courage to live according to philosophical principles. Through him, Plato reminds us of the importance of seeking truth and wisdom, regardless of the circumstances of life. The dialogue urges us to consider our own pursuit of truth and challenges us to assess whether we are truly living a philosophical life.

In a world increasingly focused on instant gratification and the pursuit of immediate pleasure, *Phaedo* emerges as a voice urging us to elevate our thoughts and transcend the ephemeral. The dialogue between Socrates and his disciples leads us into a deeply introspective exploration of life and death. Death, which is so often feared and avoided, is presented as a starting point for a higher existence—a journey that can only be undertaken after proper preparation, preparation that philosophy provides. Plato challenges us to question whether we are living meaningful lives, whether we are adequately preparing for what awaits us beyond the border of death.

What makes *Phaedo* even more intriguing is the complexity of the interactions between the characters. Socrates, known for his Socratic irony, is presented in a way that is both human and divine. His resilience in the face of death, his unwavering courage, and his persuasive ability make him one of the most captivating figures in Western philosophy. As he dialogues with his disciples, such as Phaedo and Simmias, we see the depth of the impact Socrates had on those around him, as well as the profound reverence and respect he was afforded. It is a vivid representation of the lasting influence that a philosopher can have on his followers and the importance of philosophy in shaping minds and souls.

Another notable point in *Phaedo* is how Plato addresses the duality between the body and the soul. While many in Plato's time viewed the body as a prison for the soul, the dialogue suggests a more nuanced and balanced view. The body is portrayed as an integral part of the human experience, a tool through which the soul seeks knowledge and virtue. This approach offers a valuable perspective on the relationship between earthly life and life after death, challenging the common view that philosophy concerns only the world of abstract ideas.

Furthermore, Plato's skill in creating engaging and persuasive dialogues is evident in *Phaedo*. As the characters discuss theories of the immortality of the soul and the nature of death, the reader finds themselves immersed in a world of logical argumentation and skillfully articulated rhetoric. The arguments interweave harmoniously, creating a tapestry of ideas and perspectives that challenge and inspire.

Phaedo is more than just a philosophical dialogue; it is an invitation to deep contemplation and exploration of the nature of the soul and existence. The power of this work lies in its ability to transcend the barriers of time, resonating with the contemporary reader just as it did with Socrates' ancient disciples. As we dive into the pages of this timeless dialogue, we are challenged to consider the fundamental questions that have troubled the human mind since time immemorial. The question of the immortality of the soul is central in *Phaedo*, and Plato addresses this issue masterfully. By arguing that the soul is immortal, he invites us to reflect on the nature of life and death in a way that goes beyond conventional religious beliefs. He reminds us that the pursuit of truth and wisdom is a journey that transcends the finite time of our earthly existence. Plato urges us to consider that the soul, through its quest for knowledge and virtue, is capable of transcending the finitude of the body, and thus, death is not the end but rather the beginning of a new journey.

The richness of argumentation in *Phaedo* is remarkable. Plato employs a series of rhetorical strategies to persuade his readers of the immortality of the soul, including the theory of reminiscence, in which the soul already possesses innate knowledge that is reactivated through learning, and the theory of Forms, in which ideal realities transcend the material world. These arguments intertwine harmoniously, creating a web of ideas that envelops us and challenges us to examine our own beliefs.

Moreover, *Phaedo* is a vivid reminder of the lasting impact Socrates had on philosophy. The way his disciples, including Phaedo and Simmias, admire him and deeply care about his death is a moving representation of the influence a great thinker has on those around him. Socrates personifies the quest for truth and virtue, and his courage in the face of death is inspiring. His example prompts us to consider whether we are, in fact, living philosophical lives, seeking truth and wisdom with the same intensity and dedication.

As we delve deeper into the richness of the *Phaedo* dialogue, we are confronted with the duality between the material world and the world of ideas, a recurring theme in Platonic philosophy. Plato argues that the sensible world, the one we perceive through the senses, is merely an imperfect shadow of the world of Forms, the realm of eternal and ideal realities. This distinction between the material world and the world of Forms leads us to question the nature of reality and the true essence of things. Through his dialogue with Simmias, Socrates reminds us that true philosophy is a search for the underlying reality, a search for the understanding of the Forms that shape our world.

Plato's philosophy, as expressed in *Phaedo*, is an incessant quest for knowledge and wisdom. He challenges us to seek truth, not only through logical reasoning but also through deep contemplation and introspection. He invites us to transcend the limitations of the material world and immerse ourselves in the search for ideal realities. In this sense, *Phaedo* is more than just a philosophical dialogue; it is a manual for the pursuit of truth and wisdom, a guide to a more meaningful and reflective life.

Another notable aspect of *Phaedo* is how Plato addresses the relationship between the soul and the body. While many ancient philosophers saw the body as an obstacle to the pursuit of truth and virtue, Plato offers a more balanced view. He acknowledges the importance of the body as the soul's temporary "prison," but also emphasizes that the body plays a crucial role in the search for truth. Through education and philosophical training, the soul can purify itself and free itself from the body's constraints, preparing for its journey after death. This complex and nuanced view of the relationship between the soul and the body challenges simplistic conceptions and leads us to consider the importance of balance in the pursuit of truth.

In conclusion, Plato's *Phaedo* is a work that continues to inspire and challenge readers to explore the deeper questions of human existence. Through insightful dialogues, convincing arguments, and captivating characters, Plato guides us on an intellectual journey that transcends the barriers of time. This dialogue invites us to question conventional notions about mortality, life, and death, and to seek truth and wisdom in a deeper and more meaningful way. *Phaedo* is a work that reminds us that philosophy is not just an intellectual exercise but also a search for the essence of human existence and an understanding of the meaning of life and death. It is an essential read for anyone who wishes to explore the depths of the human condition and the ceaseless pursuit of answers to the most fundamental questions of life.

5th Tetralogy

Cratylus

"Cratylus," the third work of Plato's fifth tetralogy, is a profound and thought-provoking reflection on the nature of language, semantics, and the role of names in human communication. In this philosophical dialogue, Plato guides us through an intricate labyrinth of linguistic theories, challenging our preconceptions about words and their meanings. Although it may appear to be a challenging read at first glance, "Cratylus" proves to be a work rich in thought, stimulating reflection on the power and complexity of language as a tool for understanding the world and reality.

The dialogue centers on a conversation between three main characters: Socrates, Cratylus, and Hermogenes. Socrates, the master of Socratic irony, plays his usual role of questioning and provoking thought, while Cratylus and Hermogenes represent two extremes on the spectrum of linguistic theories. Cratylus holds the view that words have an intrinsic connection to reality, arguing that names should be chosen based on their sound and similarity to the things they represent. On the other hand, Hermogenes defends the idea that names are arbitrarily established conventions by society and, therefore, have no necessary relation to what they represent.

The heart of the debate revolves around the question of whether names have an intrinsic meaning or if they are simply social conventions. Plato skillfully exposes the fallacies of both positions, leading the reader to a more nuanced understanding of the nature of language. He leads us to question whether names are truly tied to the essence of things or if they are merely labels we use to communicate with one another.

Furthermore, Plato explores the complex relationship between language, knowledge, and reality. He suggests that language plays a crucial role in the construction of knowledge and in understanding the world. Through his dialogue, he encourages us to consider how words shape our perception of reality and how the choice of words can influence our understanding of things.

"Cratylus" also touches on broader philosophical questions such as the nature of truth and the relationship between language and philosophy. Plato, through Socrates, leads us to question whether we can truly reach an accurate understanding of reality or if we are always limited by the imperfection of language.

As we delve deeper into reading "Cratylus," we are confronted with the complexity of its arguments. Plato, through Socrates, leads us through a series of examples and analogies, challenging us to consider the relationship between words and things in an increasingly profound way. He prompts us to reflect on the possibility that words may be vehicles of knowledge but also barriers to truth, depending on how we use them. Through insightful dialogues and carefully constructed arguments, Plato shows us how language is a powerful tool that shapes not only communication but also our understanding of the world.

One of the intriguing issues raised by Plato in "Cratylus" is the idea that language is a human creation that evolves over time. He reminds us that words are not fixed and unchanging but are subject to change and adaptation throughout history. This idea leads us to consider how language reflects not only the current reality but also the cultural and social evolution of human societies. In doing so, Plato encourages us to think of language as a window to the past and a tool for understanding the transformations of our civilization.

Moreover, "Cratylus" urges us to reflect on the power of language in shaping identity and subjectivity. Plato reminds us that our names are intrinsically tied to our identity and play a fundamental role in our self-understanding. He challenges us to consider how the names we are given in childhood may influence our perception of ourselves and shape our view of the world around us. This deep reflection leads us to question the complex interaction between language, identity, and human psychology.

"Cratylus" also addresses the issue of ambiguity in language, questioning whether words have unique and precise meanings or if they are subject to varied interpretations. Plato, with his characteristic skill of problematizing ideas, makes us question whether language is a reliable tool for expressing our thoughts and intentions. He challenges us to consider whether the inherent ambiguity of language is an obstacle to effective communication or if it is, in fact, a characteristic that enriches our capacity for expression.

In "Cratylus," Plato offers a thorough analysis of the nature of language that transcends its time and continues to be an essential reference in the philosophy of language to this day. The richness of the dialogue lies in how Plato addresses the complexities inherent in language, not by providing definitive answers but by guiding us to contemplate the deeper questions of human communication. The title itself, derived from the name of Cratylus, one of the characters in the dialogue, suggests the centrality of the theme of naming and the relationship between names and things. Plato, with his philosophical mastery, leads us to reflect on the possibility that language is both a reflection of reality and a construction that shapes our perception of the world.

Through the voices of Socrates, Cratylus, and Hermogenes, Plato stages an engaging and provocative debate in which different perspectives on language collide. Cratylus, who believes that names have an intrinsic relationship with the things they represent, embodies the idea that language is a faithful mirror of reality. On the other hand, Hermogenes argues that names are arbitrary conventions, the result of social agreement, and thus have no necessary connection to things. Through this intellectual clash, Plato invites us to consider whether language is a transparent reflection of the world or a filter that distorts our perception.

One of the most fascinating issues Plato raises is the possibility that language could be a tool for social control. He warns us of the power of those who control naming, as they can shape how people understand reality. This leads us to consider how the manipulation of language can be used to influence public opinion, shape ideologies, and consolidate power. Through his insightful analysis, Plato makes us reflect on how language is not only a tool for communication but also an instrument of power and control.

Another intriguing aspect of "Cratylus" is the exploration of the relationship between language and knowledge. Plato suggests that language plays a fundamental role in the construction of human knowledge. He challenges us to consider how words can carry meaning and how the choice of words we use can influence our understanding of the world. This leads us to reflect on how language is not only a means of expression but also a tool for discovery and comprehension.

As we delve deeper into the pages of "Cratylus," we are challenged to consider the role of language not only in communication but also in constructing our worldview. Plato forces us to question the relationship between names and things, and whether language is a faithful representation or a social construct. However, the philosopher does not leave us adrift in perplexity. His ability to create philosophical dialogues rich in content and depth guides us through this challenging terrain with clarity and wit, challenging us to explore fundamental questions about how language mediates our understanding of reality.

The complexity of the dialogue unfolds as Plato, through Socrates, leads us to consider the fluid and evolving nature of language. He reminds us that language is in constant transformation, adapting to the needs and values of each culture and society. This makes us question the stability of language as a vehicle for universal communication and, at the same time, challenges us to perceive how language is a living and dynamic tool that shapes and is shaped by cultural and social evolution.

One of the themes that resonates deeply in "Cratylus" is the issue of truth and accuracy in language. Plato leads us to ponder whether language can truly capture reality accurately or if we are always limited by the imperfect and ambiguous nature of words. He challenges us to question the relationship between language and truth, and whether we can truly rely on language as a trustworthy tool to convey knowledge and understand the world. This issue resonates not only in philosophy but also in epistemology and communication theory.

Moreover, Plato leads us to consider how language is intrinsically linked to individual and collective identity. Through his dialogue, he invites us to reflect on how the names we are given are not mere labels but have the power to shape our perception of who we are. This leads us to question how language plays a crucial role in shaping personal identity and in constructing cultural and social communities.

Finally, "Cratylus" challenges us to recognize the complexity of language and embrace its inherent ambiguity. Plato invites us to consider how ambiguity in language is not an obstacle to communication but a characteristic that allows for a wealth of meanings and interpretations. He encourages us to embrace this ambiguity and explore the infinite possibilities of expression that language offers.

In summary, "Cratylus" is a work of rare depth and complexity that continues to captivate and challenge readers across the centuries. Through this dialogue, Plato invites us to explore the complexities of language, truth, identity, and culture. He teaches us to embrace the ambiguity of language and appreciate its ability to shape our perceptions and our understanding of the world. Thus, "Cratylus" remains essential reading for anyone interested in the philosophy of language and in exploring the intersections between language and human existence.

Ion

"Ion," a dialogue by Plato that is part of the fifth tetralogy of his works, is a philosophical text that, despite its relative brevity, raises profound and complex questions about the nature of poetic inspiration and the authority of the poet. In this dialogue, Plato invites us into a world of questioning and debates that continue to echo through the centuries.

The dialogue begins with Socrates meeting Ion, a renowned rhapsode, at a gathering. Socrates is intrigued by Ion's ability to passionately recite and discuss Homer's poems, but his curiosity is not limited to Ion's technical skill. Socrates immediately launches a series of questions that aim to explore Ion's knowledge of other subjects, such as medicine and carpentry, and here lies the first philosophical dilemma: why is a poet skilled in a specific field not equally competent in other areas?

As the conversation unfolds, Socrates argues that Ion's ability to recite poetry is the result of a kind of "divine inspiration" that cannot be explained by the mere acquisition of knowledge. This leads us to a deeper reflection on the nature of poetry and the poet's role in society. Plato, through Socrates, raises the question of whether poets are merely passive interpreters of the muses or if they have an active role in the creation and interpretation of works.

Moreover, the discussion between Socrates and Ion also leads us to consider the question of the poet's authority. Ion believes that his ability to interpret poetry gives him authority over the subjects addressed in the poems, but Socrates challenges him, questioning whether poets really possess substantial knowledge about these subjects or if they are simply "possessed" by inspiration. This reflection prompts a critical evaluation of the society in which we live, where we often give credibility to individuals with artistic skills without questioning their actual knowledge of the subjects they address.

Another interesting point in the dialogue is the idea that poetry is contagious and can deeply influence those who hear it. Socrates argues that Ion, by reciting Homer's verses, is like a doctor who transmits diseases to others, and this analogy leads us to consider how words and art have the power to shape people's minds and actions.

As "Ion" progresses, Plato leads us to a deeper analysis of the relationship between poetry and philosophy. Socrates argues that poets, including Ion, are engaged in a form of "divine madness" that is not based on rational knowledge but on emotion and inspiration. This philosophical perspective challenges the traditional view of poetry as a source of wisdom and knowledge, suggesting that it may be a form of illusion, leading us to question the truth that resides in art.

The discussion between Socrates and Ion also raises the question of the poetry audience and how the masses react to the interpretations of poets. Socrates argues that the audience is often influenced by the poets' interpretations, and this influence can be dangerous. This makes us reflect on how poetry and rhetoric are used to persuade and manipulate the masses, a question that remains relevant today.

Furthermore, "Ion" addresses the idea that specialized knowledge is a more legitimate form of knowledge than mere opinion. Socrates argues that to be a true expert in poetry, Ion should be able to interpret all poets, not just Homer. This leads us to consider the nature of specialized knowledge and the importance of going beyond superficial opinions to obtain a deeper understanding of a field of study.

One of the most intriguing parts of the dialogue is when Socrates suggests that the true source of inspiration for poets is not knowledge, but divine madness. He compares poetic inspiration to divination and prophecy, suggesting that poets are, in a sense, intermediaries between the gods and mortals. This leads us to think about the nature of creativity and inspiration, and how they relate to the quest for truth.

As the dialogue unfolds, Plato provides us with an insightful analysis of the characteristics of the poet, particularly those who specialize in epic poetry, such as Ion. Socrates, with his typical questioning approach, seeks to understand the nature of poetic inspiration and whether it is a valid form of knowledge. It is here that we encounter the tension between reason and emotion, logic and intuition, which remains a central theme in many philosophical and artistic debates.

Through the persona of Ion, Plato shows us what it means to be in a state of poetic ecstasy, where the poet seems possessed by a divine force that drives him to recite verses with enthusiasm. This characterization of a poet as someone who transcends common knowledge and reaches a higher state of perception is fascinating. It raises the question of the origin of creativity and whether poetic inspiration is truly a form of access to a deeper and more transcendental truth.

Socrates, on the other hand, maintains a more skeptical position. He argues that the poet is not a true expert because his knowledge is unstable and uncertain, depending on a divine source that cannot be trusted. This leads us to consider the limitations of human knowledge and the complex relationship between reason and intuition. Who holds true knowledge—the inspired poet or the philosopher who seeks truth through reason?

"Ion" also invites us to reflect on the issue of intellectual authority. In an era when rhetoric and oratory played a key role in politics and education, Plato questions whether the ability to recite a poem well gives the poet real authority over the subjects addressed in the work. This question is relevant in our contemporary world, where rhetorical persuasion often outweighs solid knowledge, reminding us of the importance of questioning the source of intellectual authority.

Plato's "Ion" is a work that continues to challenge and inspire thinkers of all ages. It is an invitation to examine our beliefs, our search for truth, and our understanding of human creativity. As we explore the dialogues between Socrates and Ion, we are prompted to question the role of art and emotion in the formation of our knowledge and to consider the complexities of human nature. It is a work that remains captivating and provocative, a constant reminder that the philosophical questions raised by Plato centuries ago still resonate deeply in our contemporary world, challenging us to seek answers and deepen our understanding of the universe and ourselves.

Euthydemus

"Euthydemus," the famous work of Plato that is part of the 5th tetralogy, is a captivating philosophical dialogue that leads us into a deep reflection on the nature of sophistry and the true essence of virtue. In this text, we will dive into the complex layers of this timeless work, exploring its ideas and arguments with a critical and insightful perspective. The plot unfolds in Athens, where Socrates, Plato's intellectual protagonist, encounters two renowned sophists, Euthydemus and Dionysius. The dialogue begins seemingly innocently, with Socrates asking seemingly naive questions about the nature of virtue and wisdom. However, as the conversation progresses, we realize that Plato is guiding us through a maze of arguments and logical reasoning that challenges us to think deeply about the validity of the sophists' assertions.

One of the central issues of this dialogue is the definition of virtue and the ability to teach it. Euthydemus and Dionysius claim to be able to teach virtue, but Socrates, with his usual intellectual humility, questions the validity of their claims. He leads them through a series of complex arguments, exposing the contradictions in their positions. Through this incisive questioning, Plato urges us to think about the nature of virtue and whether it can truly be taught or if it is inherent to human nature.

Furthermore, "Euthydemus" makes us question the ethics and morality of sophistry. The sophists were known for their rhetorical skill and for selling knowledge, often in pursuit of personal interests. The dialogue invites us to reflect on the importance of intellectual honesty and the search for truth in opposition to rhetorical manipulation. Socrates reminds us that true wisdom lies in the constant search for knowledge, intellectual humility, and dedication to virtue, rather than simply persuading others with eloquent arguments. Additionally, "Euthydemus" offers a valuable critique of intellectual arrogance. The sophists, represented by Euthydemus and Dionysius, are portrayed as presumptuous and self-confident in their supposed ability to teach virtue. Socrates, on the other hand, presents us with a model of a thinker who is willing to recognize his own ignorance and constantly question his beliefs. This intellectual humility is a fundamental quality in Socratic philosophy, which Plato highlights brilliantly.

In a world filled with persuasive speeches and rhetorical manipulations, Plato's "Euthydemus" stands as a beacon of critique against intellectual vanity, the search for truth, and the essence of virtue. As we delve into this fascinating dialogue, we are confronted with a series of philosophical challenges that continue to resonate through the centuries. Socrates, the master of irony and maieutics, stands out as the intellectual protagonist who guides us through the maze of sophistic argumentation. With insightful questions, he tests the claims of Euthydemus and Dionysius that they can teach virtue. The answers given by these experienced sophists reveal their self-confidence, but also their contradictions and limitations. Through the character of Socrates, Plato challenges us to question not only what virtue is, but also whether virtue can truly be taught.

One of the central issues that emerges from this dialogue is the difference between empty rhetoric and true wisdom. The sophists, with their rhetorical skills, were often able to persuade the masses, but Socrates reminds us that persuasion is not the same as knowledge. True wisdom does not lie solely in eloquent arguments but in a deep understanding of reality and virtue. "Euthydemus" challenges us to discern between deceptive sophistry and the sincere pursuit of truth. Moreover, intellectual humility emerges as a vital theme in this work. Socrates, known for his famous phrase "I know that I know nothing," presents us with a model of a thinker who is willing to admit his own ignorance and continually investigate. This contrasts vividly with the arrogant attitude of the sophists, who see themselves as possessors of absolute knowledge. Plato urges us to recognize that the search for truth requires an open mind, free from prejudice, and the courage to question our deeply rooted beliefs.

Furthermore, "Euthydemus" leads us to reflect on the importance of ethics in the pursuit of virtue. Sophistry was often associated with the pursuit of power and wealth, to the detriment of intellectual honesty and truth. Socrates, in turn, invites us to consider virtue not as a means to a personal end, but as an end in itself. True wisdom and true virtue are intrinsically linked to integrity and honesty, reminding us that the pursuit of knowledge should be guided by a genuine desire to understand and improve ourselves and our society.

"Euthydemus," Plato's dialogue that urges us to dive into the depths of philosophy and rhetoric, continues to captivate us with its wealth of meanings and its timeless relevance. As we examine the arguments and ideas contained in this classic work, we are led to explore the complexity of the relationships between language, knowledge, virtue, and ethics.

Socrates, with his mastery in the art of questioning, guides us on an intellectual journey that challenges us to examine not only what virtue is, but also how we can achieve it. While the sophists Euthydemus and Dionysius claim to possess the knowledge to teach virtue, Socrates subtly challenges their assertions with a series of carefully constructed questions. This leads us to question the true nature of virtue and whether it can be transmitted through instruction. This in-depth exploration confronts us with the need to distinguish between mere retention of information and true understanding of fundamental ethical issues.

Another intriguing dimension of this dialogue is the critique of sophistry, which manifests not only in the pursuit of virtue but also in the manipulation of language. The sophists were masters of rhetoric and persuasion, often using their verbal skill to gain power and influence. However, Plato urges us to question whether rhetoric should be used solely for selfish purposes or if it can be a tool in the pursuit of truth. Through Socrates, he warns us of the dangers of empty persuasion and encourages us to use language in an ethical and responsible manner.

Moreover, the issue of intellectual humility remains a central and inspiring theme in "Euthydemus." Socrates, with his constant self-awareness of his own ignorance, reminds us of the importance of recognizing our limitations and being willing to learn. This intellectual humility becomes a fundamental foundation for the search for knowledge and virtue. While the sophists boast of their supposed mastery of knowledge, Socrates stands out as an example of how true wisdom begins with the admission that we still have much to learn.

"Euthydemus," one of the intellectual gems of Plato's 5th tetralogy, remains a monument to philosophical inquiry and the biting critique of empty rhetoric. As we continue analyzing this fascinating dialogue, we are enveloped by a web of complex issues that continue to echo throughout the history of philosophy and human reflection.

The search for the definition of virtue, central to "Euthydemus," drives us to explore the intricacies of ethics and morality. The main characters, Socrates, Euthydemus, and Dionysius, embark on an intellectual journey in search of understanding what virtue is and whether it can be taught.

The answers, however, are not simple, and it is precisely this complexity that makes this dialogue so engaging. Through a series of meticulous questions and logical analyses, Plato invites us to consider whether virtue is a skill that can be transmitted through teaching or if it is an intrinsic quality of human character. This reflection leads us to question not only what virtue is, but also how we can achieve it in our lives.

The critique of sophistry that permeates the dialogue is not merely a condemnation of empty rhetoric but also a deep analysis of the nature of language and knowledge. The sophists were known for their rhetorical skills, but they often used them for selfish purposes. Socrates, with his emphasis on the search for truth, reminds us that language should not merely be a tool for persuasion but a vehicle for the pursuit of genuine knowledge. "Euthydemus" invites us to consider the ethical role of language and the responsibility of those who use it to shape the minds and opinions of others.

Intellectual humility, embodied by Socrates, is a recurring theme in this work. The sophists, with their self-assured posture, contrast with Socrates, who acknowledges his own ignorance and is humble in his inquiries. This attitude of questioning one's own understanding and being willing to recognize one's own ignorance are aspects that make Socrates a beacon of critical thinking. This dialogue is a powerful reminder that true wisdom begins with the admission of one's own ignorance.

In summary, Plato's "Euthydemus" is a treasure of classical philosophy that continues to captivate, provoke, and inspire readers around the world. Through its discussions on virtue, ethics, rhetoric, and intellectual humility, Plato gifts us with an invitation to deep reflection on the meaning of truth, wisdom, and integrity. This work transcends the barriers of time and stands as an intellectual beacon, reminding us of the importance of questioning, learning, and cultivating moral and intellectual excellence in our lives.

Menexenus

Plato's dialogue "Menexenus," part of his fifth tetralogy, is a philosophical piece that stands out for its unique and provocative approach to the themes of rhetoric and oratory. In this text, Plato leads us through a deep and thought-provoking reflection on the art of persuasion and the nature of politics, revealing brilliance that echoes through the centuries.

The narrative unfolds in a peculiar setting: Socrates, the iconic philosopher, meets Menexenus, a young Athenian, and together they embark on an intellectual journey in search of understanding rhetorical practices and political discourse. The work begins with Socrates making a subtle provocation, questioning whether Menexenus is capable of delivering a speech on a subject similar to one he himself had spoken about in a funeral oration given by Aspasia. From that point, we are guided through a meticulous analysis of the tricks of rhetoric and politics as Socrates and Menexenus engage in a heated and insightful dialogue.

The great irony of the work lies in Plato's biting critique of rhetoric, a fundamental field of study in his time, while simultaneously using it to convey his own ideas. Through the words of Socrates, the author exposes the artificiality and manipulation present in the oratory of political speeches, highlighting how they are often used to win the minds of the masses, at the expense of the search for truth. It is an invitation for deep reflection on the effectiveness of rhetoric in persuading, not only through logic and solid argumentation but also through its ability to touch people's sensibilities.

One of the most intriguing aspects of "Menexenus" is how Plato addresses the role of speech in the formation of public opinion. He challenges readers to consider the responsibility of those who deliver political speeches, and how such speeches can influence the direction of society. Through the dialogue between Socrates and Menexenus, Plato makes us question whether oratory should be used as a purely persuasive tool or if there is a moral obligation to seek truth and justice in political rhetoric. Furthermore, the work also highlights the importance of education in shaping citizens. Socrates argues that true education should be based on the pursuit of wisdom and a deep understanding of matters, in contrast to the mere memorization of empty speeches. Through his character, Plato warns us of the dangers of a society that values the form of speech more than its substantial content.

As we delve deeper into "Menexenus," it is impossible not to notice Plato's ingenious use of dialogue as a philosophical tool. The author, by bringing to life the inquisitive figure of Socrates, captures the nuances of human thought and the complexities of social interactions. In this dialogue, Socrates acts as the eternal questioner, guiding the reader through a maze of questions and answers that lead to the discovery of truth. He challenges Menexenus, and by extension the reader, to critically examine rhetoric, politics, and the very nature of the quest for knowledge.

The narrative evolves intricately, as Socrates and Menexenus explore not only rhetoric but also memory and history. Plato, through Socrates, makes us consider how memory and tradition can be selectively used to influence public opinion. This discussion is notably relevant today when the manipulation of information and the fabrication of history can profoundly impact politics and society.

Another notable aspect of "Menexenus" is the critique of the superficiality and formalism present in the oratory of its time. Plato, through Socrates, emphasizes the importance of diving deeper into issues, rather than relying on empty rhetorical formulas. He reminds us that true persuasion cannot be achieved solely with a command of words, but with a genuine commitment to truth and justice.

As we continue reading, we are confronted with a provocative reflection on the nature of democracy and politics. Socrates questions whether democracy, as practiced in Athens at his time, was truly the most just political system. He makes us reflect on how rhetoric is often used to manipulate the masses and ensure that the interests of the few prevail over those of the many. The "Menexenus" invites us to think about the eternal challenges of democracy and citizen participation, casting a critical eye on the political practices of ancient Greece and provoking a deep analysis of contemporary politics.

At the core of this work, we find a fundamental question that continues to echo in our hearts and minds: what is the responsibility of citizens in shaping a just and wise society? Plato, through his teacher Socrates, argues that the pursuit of truth and justice should be the ultimate goal of rhetoric and politics. It is a timeless reminder that rhetoric, when used correctly, can be a powerful tool for good, for educating minds, and for forming responsible and just citizens.

As we deepen our analysis of "Menexenus," it is remarkable how Plato, through his masterful use of dialogue, constructs a narrative that transcends the barriers of time and culture. Socrates' ability to question and challenge social and intellectual conventions resonates with a disturbing relevance, and it is this timeless aspect that makes this work a philosophical treasure.

One of the most intriguing features of "Menexenus" is its rich tapestry of interconnected themes, including rhetoric, memory, history, democracy, and justice. These elements intertwine in a complex way, revealing Plato's profound vision of human nature and society. The dialogue makes us question not only what is said but how it is said, and more importantly, why. Through the confrontation between Socrates and Menexenus, the author leads us to consider the ethical and moral implications of our words and actions, as well as the fundamental role of education in forming responsible and just citizens.

Regarding rhetoric, Plato critically examines persuasion as a political tool. He challenges us to look beyond the brilliant words and empty promises, and to question the intentions behind speeches. "Menexenus" is a call to action for us to be critical citizens, capable of discerning between true and deceptive discourse, between the sincere search for truth and calculated manipulation.

The dialogue also emphasizes the importance of memory and history in shaping public opinion. In an era where information is consumed voraciously and often out of context, Plato's work invites us to consider how selective memory and historical narrative can be used for political ends. He warns us of the need for a critical approach to the construction of collective memory, highlighting how the manipulation of history can serve particular interests.

The reflection on democracy, central to the "Menexenus" dialogue, remains an undeniably relevant topic. Plato, through Socrates, questions whether democracy as we know it is the most just political system or if it is susceptible to corruption and demagoguery. These inquiries echo in our own era, where democracy faces constant challenges, and the need for informed and engaged citizens is more pressing than ever.

In summary, Plato's "Menexenus" is a work of inexhaustible richness that invites us on a journey of self-discovery and reflection on rhetoric, politics, and ethics. It is a demonstration of the enduring capacity of Platonic philosophy to illuminate the perennial challenges of the human condition. This work remains a beacon of wisdom, guiding us in the eternal search for knowledge, justice, and truth.

6th Tetralogy

Parmenides

"Parmenides," one of Plato's most intriguing philosophical dialogues, is part of the sixth tetralogy of his works and delves deeply into the issues of existence, being, and reality. In this dialogue, Plato takes us on a challenging intellectual journey, where Parmenides, a renowned Eleatic philosopher, engages in a discussion with the young Socrates, raising questions that challenge traditional conceptions of reality and knowledge.

The structure of the "Parmenides" dialogue is notably complex and, in some ways, bold. It begins with a meeting between Socrates and Parmenides, in which Socrates expresses his admiration for the famous Eleatic philosopher. Soon, Parmenides assumes the role of mentor and begins questioning Socrates about his philosophical beliefs. The dialogue unfolds into a series of meticulously crafted arguments and counterarguments that explore the nature of reality, the relationship between the One and the Many, and the question of knowledge. It is a challenging intellectual journey, in which Plato invites us to question our own convictions and consider the complexities of philosophy.

One of the most notable features of "Parmenides" is the way Plato presents the idea that the One, the absolute unity, is the only true reality, and that the sensible world, full of multiplicity and change, is an illusion. Parmenides argues persuasively that reality cannot be multiple, as plurality involves division and therefore cannot be absolutely real. This view challenges conventional notions of how we perceive the world around us, leading us to a deep reflection on the nature of existence.

However, Plato does not present Parmenides as an unshakable and infallible philosopher. He also highlights the limitations of Parmenides himself, who hesitates in his reasoning and acknowledges the complexity of the issues being discussed. This adds a layer of realism to the dialogue, reminding us that philosophy is an ongoing and often confusing quest for knowledge.

Furthermore, "Parmenides" challenges us to consider the relationship between philosophy and dialectics. Dialectics is a technique of argumentation that Plato often employs in his dialogues, where characters debate logically and systematically. In "Parmenides," we see Parmenides and Socrates engaged in a sophisticated discussion, questioning and exploring abstract ideas and complex concepts. This reminds us that philosophy is not just a quest for definitive answers but also a process of constant questioning and investigation.

As we delve deeper into reading "Parmenides," the work grows in complexity and depth, challenging our previous conceptions and inviting us to rethink what we thought we knew about the world and reality. As Parmenides and Socrates continue their discussion, the arguments become more intricate, and dialectics takes center stage, demonstrating Plato's skill in creating a dialogue that is both a work of philosophy and a high-level intellectual exercise.

One of the most memorable passages in the dialogue occurs when Parmenides guides Socrates through a series of contradictory arguments, pointing out that if we accept the idea of the One as the only true reality, we are forced to conclude that the sensible world is not real. However, this raises the question of how we can explain the apparent multiplicity and change we experience in our everyday reality. This section of the dialogue is a true exercise in reflection, challenging us to reconcile the apparent contradictions in our conceptions of reality.

Plato also invites us to consider the relationship between philosophy and metaphysics. In the "Parmenides" dialogue, we see how the search for knowledge intertwines with profound questions about the nature of existence and reality. Parmenides, with his view that the One is the only true reality, raises questions that transcend mere epistemology and lead us to the heart of metaphysics. These profound philosophical questions continue to be a source of discussion and debate in contemporary philosophy, demonstrating the timelessness and relevance of Plato's dialogue.

Moreover, "Parmenides" challenges us to think about the role of the philosopher in the pursuit of knowledge. Parmenides is portrayed as a master who guides Socrates through a complex and challenging intellectual territory. This raises the question of how knowledge is transmitted and acquired in philosophy, and how the relationship between master and pupil plays a crucial role in the process of philosophical inquiry. The dynamic between Parmenides and Socrates reminds us that philosophy is a living tradition of the pursuit of knowledge, in which dialogue and interaction between philosophers play a central role.

As we delve even further into the depths of Plato's "Parmenides," we encounter an intellectual exercise that goes beyond mere theoretical questions. The dialogue reminds us that in philosophy, ideas are often not presented as ready-made truths, but as tools for exploring thought and reality. Parmenides' hesitation in his own arguments shows that philosophy is a field in which uncertainty and questioning are inherent, where definitive answers are often elusive. This invites us to adopt an attitude of intellectual humility, recognizing that the pursuit of knowledge often involves more questions than answers.

One of the central questions that Plato addresses in "Parmenides" is the relationship between the world of ideas and the sensible world. Parmenides argues that the One, as the supreme and unifying idea, is the only true reality, while the sensible world is an illusion. This leads us to consider the nature of ideas in Plato and how they relate to the world we perceive through the senses. The dialogue challenges us to explore how abstract ideas can be the source of the reality we experience, and how philosophy can help us understand the complexities of this relationship.

Furthermore, "Parmenides" invites us to consider the role of dialectics in philosophy. Dialectics, as presented in this dialogue, is a powerful tool that allows for the systematic exploration of complex ideas. Parmenides and Socrates use dialectics to analyze and test philosophical hypotheses in a methodical and rigorous way. This reminds us that philosophy is not an exercise in mere abstract thinking but a process of careful and critical investigation, in which ideas are subjected to thorough scrutiny.

In the pages of "Parmenides," Plato leads us through a philosophical labyrinth, where knowledge and reality unfold before our eyes in a complex dance of arguments and counterarguments. The dialogue, often considered enigmatic, reveals its richness as we are guided through the layers of meaning. Each twist in the discussion between Parmenides and Socrates is like a challenge to our ability to comprehend, inviting us to consider how our own ideas about the world fit into this philosophical puzzle.

The "Parmenides" dialogue also highlights the importance of language in philosophy. Through the careful use of language, Parmenides and Socrates explore complex concepts and metaphysical abstractions. They unearth the underlying meanings of words and analyze the structure of discourse, showing how language plays a crucial role in the formulation and communication of knowledge. This emphasis on language reminds us that philosophy is not just a quest for ideas but also an exploration of the power and limitations of language as a tool for thought.

One of the most striking characteristics of "Parmenides" is the way Plato presents Parmenides not just as a wise philosopher, but as a human figure with his own uncertainties and hesitations. As Parmenides progresses in his argument, he acknowledges the complexities of the issues he is exploring and shows a genuine willingness to engage in intellectual inquiry. This reminds us that philosophy is not a quest for absolute truths, but rather a process of search, questioning, and constant reflection.

As we become more immersed in the web of arguments and counterarguments presented in "Parmenides," we realize that Plato is not just exposing philosophical theories, but also exploring the very act of philosophizing. The dialogue invites us to contemplate how the human mind reaches out toward the abyss of knowledge, how we attempt to grasp the ungraspable and conceive the inconceivable. Parmenides and Socrates are like two fearless navigators searching for unknown lands, and as they venture forth, they lead us to question the nature of our own search for truth and wisdom.

One of the most intriguing features of "Parmenides" is Plato's ability to create an atmosphere of intense reflection and speculation. As the arguments unfold, we are invited to consider the profound implications of the ideas discussed. Plato challenges us to explore the limits of human thought, to enter unknown intellectual territories, and to confront the unknown. This brings us back to the essence of philosophy, which is, ultimately, an unrelenting pursuit of understanding and truth.

Another notable aspect of "Parmenides" is the way it forces us to confront the contradictions and paradoxes that arise throughout the discussion. Parmenides presents a series of contradictory arguments that seem to undermine his own conclusions. These contradictions remind us that philosophy is not a quest for an absolute and unquestionable truth, but an exploration of complex ideas and concepts. Through the analysis of contradictions, Plato invites us to an exercise of self-criticism and self-reflection, reinforcing the idea that philosophy is a constant search for the refinement of thought.

Finally, "Parmenides" is a work that, more than any other, reminds us that philosophy is an incessant and passionate pursuit of knowledge. It is a dialogue that challenges us to explore the deepest recesses of our minds, to question our most fundamental assumptions, and to embrace the complexity inherent in the search for truth. Plato invites us to embark on an intellectual journey that is both stimulating and challenging, and that continues to be an inexhaustible source of inspiration for all those who venture to explore the depths of philosophy. "Parmenides" is, without a doubt, one of the jewels of human thought, a work that will remain relevant and captivating for centuries, continuing to illuminate the path of the search for knowledge and wisdom.

Theaetetus

"Theaetetus," one of the most influential works by the Greek philosopher Plato, is a philosophical dialogue found in the 6th tetralogy, renowned for its richness in ideas and depth of analysis. Through a conversation between Socrates and Theaetetus, Plato delves into the deep waters of knowledge, epistemology, and the nature of human thought. In this critical review, we will explore the main issues addressed in this work and how it continues to challenge readers' minds to this day.

The first characteristic that stands out in "Theaetetus" is Socrates' approach through the dialectical method. Socrates, the philosophical protagonist in Plato's dialogues, begins the conversation with Theaetetus by asking carefully crafted questions, leading the young man to reflect on what knowledge is and how it can be attained. This method, known as the Socratic method or maieutics, is a powerful tool Plato uses to explore his disciple's ideas.

The core of the discussion revolves around the question: "What is knowledge?". Socrates and Theaetetus debate various definitions, such as true justified belief and perception. However, the dialogue does not reach a definitive conclusion. This lack of resolution is one of the most intriguing elements of the work, as Plato leaves the question open-ended, inviting readers to continue the pursuit of understanding. This reminds us that philosophy does not settle for easy answers but seeks the truth in a constant and tireless manner.

Another notable aspect of "Theaetetus" is the exploration of the relationship between knowledge and sensation. Plato questions whether sensory perception is a reliable source of knowledge or if it is illusory. This discussion remains relevant today, as neuroscience and philosophy of mind continue to explore how we perceive the world around us. Plato anticipated many of these issues, demonstrating his remarkable ability to think ahead of his time.

Furthermore, "Theaetetus" also addresses the importance of precise definitions of words and concepts. Socrates argues that, in order to achieve true knowledge, we must be able to clearly define our concepts. This emphasizes the importance of language and logic in philosophy, an idea that remains fundamental in contemporary philosophy. However, "Theaetetus" is not just a dense philosophical treatise but also a dialogue that reveals human nature. The figure of Theaetetus, a young man eager to learn and willing to face intellectual challenges, reflects the spirit of learning and the pursuit of knowledge. The very existence of Theaetetus as a character is a tribute to the crucial role of disciples in philosophy, showing how knowledge is transmitted and perpetuated across generations.

The search for knowledge in "Theaetetus" transcends the limitations of time and space, persisting as an intellectual beacon that illuminates curious minds. The dialogue is not confined to mere theoretical speculation but delves into the essence of human experience and the way we understand the world around us. Through his characters, Plato challenges us to explore the complexities of the mind and thought, inviting us to look beyond the surface of things and question the truths we take for granted.

One of the most remarkable features of "Theaetetus" is the representation of philosophy as a dynamic and collaborative process. The dialogue between Socrates and Theaetetus is not a doctrinal monologue but an ongoing intellectual exchange. Plato shows us the importance of dialogue and debate in the search for knowledge, highlighting that truth often emerges from the confrontation of ideas and critical reflection. This emphasis on collaboration and continuous questioning is a valuable lesson for all philosophy students and, indeed, for anyone in search of wisdom.

Additionally, "Theaetetus" also reminds us of the humility required in the search for knowledge. Throughout the dialogue, Socrates acknowledges that knowledge is fleeting and elusive, and the quest for truth is an endless journey. This contrasts with the intellectual arrogance often found in contemporary society, where people tend to believe they have all the answers. Plato invites us to embrace uncertainty and to view the pursuit of knowledge as an ongoing process of self-improvement.

Another fascinating aspect of "Theaetetus" is Plato's critique of sophistry, a contemporary philosophical movement that sought to manipulate rhetoric to persuade and convince, often at the cost of truth. Through Socrates, Plato refutes sophistic notions of knowledge, highlighting the importance of the search for objective truth and rational justification. This conflict between philosophy and sophistry resonates today, when we are confronted with the spread of misleading information and the manipulation of rhetoric in politics and media.

"Theaetetus" by Plato, in the 6th tetralogy, is thus a work that challenges us to go beyond appearances and explore the depths of thought. Socrates and Theaetetus remind us that true knowledge cannot simply be a casual belief or an uncritical acceptance of the information presented to us. True wisdom requires us to ask difficult questions and to challenge our own conceptions. Like Theaetetus, we are all students in an eternal process of learning, and the journey toward knowledge is as valuable as the truth itself.

Another notable aspect of "Theaetetus" is how Plato leads us to reflect on the nature of reality. Through the dialogue, he makes us question whether the reality perceived by our senses is the only reality. This questioning echoes in contemporary discussions about the nature of reality, such as quantum physics theories, which challenge our conventional understanding of the world. Plato anticipated these issues, demonstrating that philosophy is not static, but dynamic and constantly evolving, keeping pace with the progress of human knowledge.

"Theaetetus" also inspires us to consider the role of reason in the search for knowledge. Socrates argues that reason is the key to true understanding, and rational justification is essential for the acquisition of knowledge. This emphasis on reason resonates with the philosophical tradition that extends from Plato's time to contemporary debates on epistemology and logic. The importance of reason as a fundamental tool in the pursuit of truth is a timeless lesson that "Theaetetus" imparts.

Moreover, Plato's work also invites us to explore the ethical dimensions of knowledge. The dialogue is not only an intellectual investigation but also an exploration of the moral implications of our beliefs and actions. Socrates reminds us that knowledge is inseparable from virtue, and the pursuit of knowledge must be accompanied by an equally fervent quest for wisdom and moral excellence. This ethical dimension of philosophy is a fundamental part of Plato's legacy, continuing to inspire those who seek not only understanding but also a dignified and just life.

In summary, Plato's "Theaetetus" is a work of profound relevance and captivating complexity. Through insightful dialogues, incisive questioning, and a comprehensive exploration of fundamental issues of knowledge, Plato invites us on an intellectual journey that transcends the limitations of time and space. The legacy of "Theaetetus" is the celebration of the pursuit of knowledge as a noble and unrelenting act that challenges us to look beyond appearances, embrace uncertainty, and relentlessly seek the truth. As a gem of Western philosophy, this work continues to shine as a beacon of wisdom, guiding those who venture to explore the depths of human thought.

The Sophist

The Sophist, written by Plato and part of the 6th tetralogy of his works, is a philosophical piece known for its depth and complexity in the issues it addresses. In this dialogue, Plato presents a thorough investigation into the concept of the sophist, a term debated in ancient Greece and still relevant today. With his unique mastery, the Athenian philosopher constructs a philosophical setting in which Socrates and a young foreigner seek to define and distinguish the sophist, exploring sophistry and its relationship with philosophy.

One of the most intriguing aspects of *The Sophist* is the way Plato leads the discussion, revealing the inherent traps of the art of rhetoric. Through Socrates, the philosopher questions the sophists about the nature of wisdom, the difference between true knowledge and persuasive speech, making truth relative to the observer. This is particularly relevant today, where rhetoric and persuasion play crucial roles in politics, media, and society. Plato also addresses the issue of ontology, exploring the nature of reality and being. The distinction between being and non-being, existence and non-existence, is examined, prompting the reader to reflect on knowledge and reality. Through carefully constructed arguments, Plato challenges our preconceived notions of what is real.

Another fascinating aspect of the dialogue is Plato's critique of eristic dialectic, the art of arguing deceptively. He demonstrates how sophists use speech to create an illusion of truth, promoting false ideas. This critique is a timeless warning about the dangers of rhetorical manipulation and the lack of intellectual sincerity. Plato also explores the relationship between philosophy and politics, suggesting that true philosophy seeks the common good and justice, while sophists often seek only power and personal gain. This discussion continues to resonate today as we face political and ethical challenges in our society.

As we delve into the pages of *The Sophist* and absorb its wealth of content, we are confronted with a central dilemma that echoes through the ages: the quest for truth and wisdom in contrast to rhetorical manipulation. Through the dialogue between Socrates and the young foreigner, Plato leads us to reflect on the nature of language and argumentation, questioning whether persuasion is a reliable means of seeking knowledge. The tricks of rhetoric and the ability to persuade with convincing arguments, often devoid of real substance, are meticulously dissected.

The depth of Plato's investigation goes beyond mere criticism of sophistry and eristic dialectic. It delves into ontology, exploring the relationship between being and non-being, existence and non-existence. Plato challenges us to consider reality in its most fundamental form, questioning how we can know the truth in a world where appearances often deceive. This philosophical inquiry is essential for our ongoing quest for understanding, prompting us to question not only the validity of rhetorical arguments but also the very nature of the reality around us.

As we follow Socrates and the young foreigner in their investigation, we realize that the distinction between true knowledge and false wisdom becomes increasingly crucial. Plato warns us about the dangers of accepting arguments based solely on superficial persuasion, encouraging us to seek truth through critical thinking and reason.

Moreover, *The Sophist* offers a view of the intricate relationship between philosophy and politics. Plato suggests that true philosophy is intrinsically tied to justice and the common good, while sophists often serve personal interests and power. This discussion strongly resonates in today's society, where complex ethical and political issues are at stake, and Plato's reflections on the relationship between philosophy and politics are more relevant than ever.

The wealth of ideas presented in *The Sophist* is a celebration of the human mind's ability to transcend the limitations of time and space. As we dive deeper into the work, we are challenged to question our understanding of the world and reconsider the foundations of our beliefs. Plato's dialogue serves as a beacon of wisdom, guiding us in exploring the depths of philosophy and inspiring us to relentlessly seek truth.

Reading Plato's *The Sophist* is an invitation to a profound intellectual journey, where ideas interweave like threads in a complex philosophical puzzle. In this dialogue, Plato skillfully guides us through the intricate issues of rhetoric, ontology, and ethics. Socrates, our guide through this maze of arguments, leads us through a labyrinth of questions, where the boundaries between knowledge and ignorance become blurred, and where language, despite its apparent ability to convey truths, can be a source of obscurity and deceit.

The question of language is a central theme in *The Sophist*. Plato encourages us to reflect on how words are used to express concepts and transmit knowledge, but also to persuade and manipulate. The sophists' ability to create persuasive arguments, often lacking substance, raises profound questions about the reliability of language as a vehicle for truth. This reflection on the nature of language is critically important in a world where rhetoric plays a central role in shaping opinions and influencing human actions.

Another key point is the exploration of ontology, the investigation of the nature of being and reality. Plato takes us on a journey that makes us question what is real and what is illusory. The distinction between being and non-being, existence and non-existence, is an enigma that resonates deeply. This leads us to consider whether the world we perceive with our senses is the entirety of reality or if there is a realm of eternal truths beyond appearances.

Additionally, *The Sophist* challenges us to examine the ethics of argumentation and rhetoric. Plato highlights the importance of intellectual integrity, showing how rhetorical manipulation can be used to gain power and influence at the cost of truth. This compels us to question not only what we say but how we say it, and how our words can shape the reality around us.

In this dialogue, Plato presents the world of ideas and invites us to consider the relationship between the world of ideal forms and the sensible world. He urges us to reflect on the pursuit of truth and wisdom as a journey that transcends appearances and seeks the essence of things. In our age of abundant information and conflicting opinions, *The Sophist* serves as a guiding beacon, reminding us of the importance of the search for truth and the need to discern between empty rhetoric and substantial knowledge.

In summary, Plato's *The Sophist,* part of the 6th tetralogy, is a philosophical work that continues to intrigue and inspire readers across generations. Its deep and rigorous exploration of rhetoric, ontology, and ethics invites profound reflection and the search for truth. Plato challenges us to consider the complexities of language and argumentation, to question the nature of knowledge and reality, and to explore the ethical implications of our interactions with the world. Ultimately, *The Sophist* is a masterpiece of philosophy that reminds us that the pursuit of wisdom is an infinite journey, an eternal quest for understanding in a world often obscured by superficial discourse and illusions.

Political

"Political" is one of Plato's philosophical masterpieces, forming an integral part of his 6th tetralogy. This treatise echoes through the centuries, provoking deep reflections on the functioning of society and the nature of government. In this dialogue, Plato takes us on an intellectual journey where we are confronted with fundamental questions that still resonate in the contemporary political landscape. With a sharp mind and impeccable rhetorical skill, the philosopher leads us to question the foundations of politics, the authority of the ruler, and the relationship between power and justice.

The first impression we have when entering the pages of "Political" is the richness of the debate and the depth of the ideas presented. Plato, as a master of dialectic, uses the dialogue as a tool to explore knowledge. The meeting between Socrates and an Athenian stranger, who acts as the interlocutor, guides us through a philosophical territory filled with challenges and inquiries. Plato's words unfold in an intricate debate about what constitutes the art of governing and how this art is connected with justice. The dialogue is a true duel of brilliant minds, an intellectual dance that challenges the reader to follow along and engage.

One of the main themes explored in "Political" is the nature of the ideal ruler. Throughout the dialogue, Plato suggests that the true ruler must be a philosopher-king, someone endowed with wisdom, virtue, and a love of truth. He argues that politics should not be left in the hands of demagogues or those who seek power for the sake of power. The emphasis on the importance of knowledge and morality in political leadership is an idea that resonates deeply in our times, in an era where political manipulation and lack of integrity are recurring issues.

The relationship between power and justice is also a central theme in "Political." Plato challenges us to question whether government should be merely a matter of force and control, or whether it should be permeated by ethical principles. He defends the idea that true justice is inextricably linked to wisdom and virtue, and that government should be a manifestation of this justice. This discussion resonates in our times, where the search for equity and social justice continues to be a hot topic of debate.

Furthermore, "Political" also makes us reflect on the complex issue of classifying political regimes. Plato draws a kind of genealogical tree of regimes, ranging from aristocracy to tyranny, and forces us to consider the advantages and disadvantages of each form of government. This leads us to reflect on how modern societies can learn from the lessons of the past and seek to improve their political structures.

Plato's "Political," an integral part of his 6th tetralogy, stands out as a work that transcends the barriers of time and space, unfolding as a timeless intellectual treasure. The depth of ideas and the mastery of argumentation present in this work continue to challenge us, making us question the foundations of politics and the essence of leadership. By leading us through a vigorous dialogue between Socrates and an Athenian stranger, Plato offers us a philosophical feast in which ideas are served in a constant flow, stimulating our minds and encouraging an incessant search for truth.

The figure of the philosopher-king emerges as a central element in Plato's discourse in "Political." He argues that the ideal ruler must be someone who is, above all, a lover of wisdom, someone who does not seek power for its own sake, but views it as a burden to be borne for the common good. This vision not only questions conventional politics, where ambition often outweighs wisdom, but also challenges citizens themselves to reflect on the kind of leadership they want for their society. Plato makes us consider the importance of virtue and knowledge in political decision-making, a call that continues to resonate in a world where integrity often gives way to greed and opportunism.

The intrinsic relationship between power and justice is another theme that powerfully echoes in "Political." Plato argues that government should be a manifestation of true justice, and that power should be exercised based on ethical principles. At a time in history when modern democracies frequently face dilemmas about justice, equity, and equality, Plato's words acquire new relevance. His appeal to ethics in politics resonates as a persistent echo, reminding us that power without moral principles is a threat to society.

The classification of political regimes, which Plato meticulously outlines in his dialogue, leads us to question the advantages and disadvantages of each form of government. By tracing a line from aristocracy to tyranny, the philosopher challenges us to consider the fate of our own societies and to seek continuous improvement. He urges us to look to the past for valuable lessons and to apply this knowledge to shape the future. "Political" makes us realize that politics is a discipline that requires constant reflection and adjustment, a timely reminder in a constantly evolving world.

As we delve deeper into the pages of "Political," we are confronted with an impressive vision of political philosophy that Plato offers us. His approach, so rich in nuance, leads us to consider the practical implications of his theories, challenging us to think not only in abstract terms but also to apply these concepts in our own lives and societies. Plato's ability to transcend the barriers of time, anticipating political issues that remain relevant today, is a testament to his genius.

The work "Political" is, in many ways, a call to action for the citizens of any era. Plato invites us to be critical, to question authority, to evaluate leaders, and to participate actively in shaping our own political destiny. The message he conveys is clear: politics should not be left in the hands of a few privileged individuals, but should be a concern for all. At a time when civic participation and political engagement are so vital, Plato's words echo as an urgent call for us to take responsibility for our own future.

The richness of the ideas contained in Plato's "Political" also challenges us to seek the balance between theory and practice in politics. While the dialogue is filled with complex philosophical theories, Plato also reminds us that politics is a practical discipline, involving action and implementation. This holistic approach encourages us to consider how we can translate philosophical ideals into concrete policies and actions, a challenge that remains crucial in our contemporary world.

Plato's ability to challenge conventional conceptions and shed light on complex political issues is evident on every page of "Political." His exploration of the relationship between the individual, the community, and the government, as well as his vision of the formation of laws and institutions, continues to inspire intellectual debates and shape political discussions. As we engage with Plato's ideas, we are confronted with the need to reevaluate our own beliefs and seek a deeper understanding of how politics affects society as a whole.

By uncovering the layers of meaning present in Plato's "Political," we encounter the profound vision of a philosopher who did not merely contemplate the world from his ivory tower but who relentlessly sought to apply his philosophical insights to the political reality. It is in this encounter between the abstract and the concrete that Plato challenges us to seek a balance between theory and practice, a dilemma that resonates intensely in our modern world, where the division between academics and politicians often seems insurmountable.

Plato's work reminds us that philosophy is not only an intellectual discipline but a compass that guides our actions and decisions. His concept of the philosopher-king, someone who unites wisdom with political action, instigates us to seek leaders who not only understand ethical principles but who also embody them in their actions. This leads us to reflect on the role of citizens in selecting and supporting leaders who embody these virtues, a civic duty that carries weight in modern democracies.

The relationship between power and justice, masterfully explored by Plato, remains an unavoidable theme in our current society. In a world where the quest for social justice is an ongoing struggle, the philosopher's words resonate as a beacon illuminating the way. He reminds us that power devoid of ethics is a danger, and that justice must be the foundation upon which politics stands. His call for integrity and morality in the political sphere is an urgent reminder for us to rethink our systems and values.

The classification of political regimes that Plato performs in his dialogue offers us a valuable lens through which we can analyze the complexities of modern political structures. His insights into the advantages and disadvantages of different forms of government force us to consider how we can shape our institutions to better meet the needs of an ever-evolving society. His writings urge us to learn from the past, while looking to the future with the intention of building fairer and more effective political systems.

Plato, with his tireless quest for a more just society and a more ethical politics, remains an intellectual beacon that illuminates the complexities of the political world and challenges us to transcend the status quo. "Political" is a work that transcends its time, sparking timeless reflections on the nature of power, leadership, and justice. As we turn its pages, we are reminded that philosophy is not merely an academic discipline but a living force that influences how we organize our societies and make political decisions.

The figure of the philosopher-king, so eloquently outlined by Plato, makes us question the type of leadership we seek. His vision of a wise and virtuous ruler, someone who puts the well-being of the community above their own interests, remains a noble and challenging aspiration. It is a call for us, as citizens, not to settle for leaders who only seek power but to demand leaders who are motivated by wisdom, the search for truth, and the promotion of the common good.

The relationship between power and justice, deeply explored by Plato, leads us to reflect on the power structures in our own societies, especially at a time when issues of equality, equity, and justice occupy the center of political debates. Plato's words echo as a reminder of the importance of ensuring that the exercise of power is intrinsically linked to ethical principles. The lesson he offers us is clear: justice cannot be mere rhetoric but must be the foundation upon which our political institutions are built.

The classification of political regimes presented by Plato, ranging from aristocracy to tyranny, challenges us to consider political structures from a new perspective. As we explore the advantages and disadvantages of each form of government, we are encouraged to critically evaluate the functioning of our own democracies. Plato invites us to learn from history, to draw valuable lessons from past civilizations, and to apply those lessons in building fairer and more effective societies.

In conclusion, Plato's "Political," part of the 6th tetralogy, transcends its time and remains a source of inspiration and reflection in our contemporary world. Through its exploration of the complexities of politics, leadership, and justice, Plato challenges us to seek a more just society, a wiser government, and a more ethical world. His work is a constant invitation to action, reflection, and the pursuit of truth, justice, and wisdom in politics, resonating as powerfully today as in Plato's time. Therefore, "Political" is not just a philosophical work; it is a call to transformation, a guide in the constant search for political and societal improvement, a light that guides us on the eternal journey toward a more just and virtuous world.

7th Tetralogy

Philebus

Plato's dialogue *Philebus*, part of the seventh tetralogy of his works, provides a fascinating philosophical exploration that leads us into a profound reflection on the pursuit of pleasure and the nature of the good. With rhetorical mastery, Plato weaves a narrative that engages the reader from the first words, guiding them through an intricate labyrinth of complex and profound ideas. Throughout this work, the Athenian philosopher challenges us to contemplate the role of pleasure in our lives, highlighting the complexities and paradoxes that arise when trying to define what is truly good.

The dialogue *Philebus* unfolds through a conversation between Philebus, Protarchus, and Socrates, in which they discuss the greatest form of good for humanity. The discussion centers on the relationship between pleasure and the highest good, a theme that remains relevant and pertinent even today. Plato, through Socrates, questions the hedonistic view that places pleasure at the center of the human pursuit, confronting it with the idea that pleasure alone cannot be considered the highest good.

The richness of *Philebus* lies in the way Plato exposes the limitations of hedonism, demonstrating that uncontrolled pleasure can result in an empty and unsatisfactory life. He argues that the unrestrained pursuit of pleasure, without ethical criteria, can lead to excesses and vices that ultimately harm the soul and the pursuit of the highest good. Through a meticulously crafted argument, Plato challenges us to consider whether pleasure, when excessive, becomes a form of suffering, and whether the pursuit of the good must be balanced with temperance and wisdom.

In this dialogue, Plato demonstrates his mastery of the art of dialectic, guiding the characters through a series of arguments and counterarguments, urging the reader to deeply reflect on the topics discussed. He incites us to question our own beliefs about pleasure and the good, as well as to evaluate whether we are truly seeking a genuinely fulfilling and virtuous life.

Philebus also emphasizes the importance of philosophy as an essential tool in the quest for knowledge and wisdom. Through Socrates' lucid arguments and meticulous analyses, Plato reminds us that philosophical reflection is fundamental to understanding the deeper questions of human existence. He invites us to question the world around us and to seek answers that go beyond superficial appearances.

In this singular dialogue, Plato also presents an intricate view of the relationship between mathematics and philosophy. He addresses the question of pleasure not only in the human context but also in the realm of knowledge and the search for truth. Through the metaphor of measurement, he suggests that mathematics plays a fundamental role in the pursuit of the highest good. Plato argues that mathematics, by dealing with measure and proportion, leads us to a deeper understanding of the order and harmony underlying the universe. This seemingly abstract perspective is crucial for Plato, as he believes that contemplating mathematical order leads us to contemplate the highest good, distancing us from unrestrained hedonistic inclinations.

Philebus also prompts us to consider the role of friendship in the pursuit of the good. According to Plato, friendship is a powerful force that can guide our choices and influence our search for the good. He explores how friendship can be a link between pleasure and virtue when based on truth and wisdom, helping us in the pursuit of what is truly good. Thus, friendship becomes a crucial element in the equation of the search for the highest good.

The depth of the ideas presented in *Philebus* is remarkable. Plato challenges us to transcend purely hedonistic concerns and to seek a balance between pleasure and wisdom, measure and mathematics, friendship and the pursuit of truth. His reasoning is logical and rigorous, yet also filled with emotion and passion for philosophy, making the reading of this dialogue a truly enriching experience.

Furthermore, the work reminds us of the importance of authenticity in the pursuit of the good. Plato encourages us to be true to ourselves, to reflect on our desires and motivations, and to seek the truth about what truly brings us happiness and satisfaction. This involves questioning the social and cultural norms that often lead us in directions contrary to our own well-being. Thus, *Philebus* becomes a call for authenticity and introspection, inviting us to look within our souls in search of what is truly valuable.

The beauty of Plato's philosophy lies not only in its ability to explore abstract concepts and metaphysical issues but also in its capacity to make these complex ideas accessible and relevant to everyday life. *Philebus* is a testament to this ability. Throughout the dialogue, Plato not only challenges us to reflect on abstract questions but also invites us to examine our own lives and choices, considering how we can apply the lessons learned from this pursuit of the highest good to our daily lives.

The dialogue also highlights the inherently dialectical nature of philosophy, where ideas are constantly questioned and revised. Plato does not seek to impose a single view of the highest good but invites us to actively participate in the process of search and reflection. He reminds us that philosophical truth is not static but dynamic, subject to continuous revision and deepening. It is a powerful reminder that philosophy is an intellectual journey, not merely a search for definitive answers.

Plato's writing in *Philebus* is skilled and captivating, with clarity that makes complex ideas accessible to the reader. His ability to create engaging dialogues, in which characters discuss ideas vividly and persuasively, is one of the reasons his works continue to be widely read and studied today. The narrative is fluid and engaging, and the richness of the arguments presented makes the reader feel immersed in the discussions, as though actively participating in the philosophical debate.

In the search for understanding the highest good, Plato challenges us to consider the fundamental question of the purpose of human existence. *Philebus* makes us reflect on what we are truly seeking in life and what the ultimate goal of our efforts and aspirations is. Plato argues that if pleasure and the unchecked pursuit of pleasure are the only goals of life, we risk falling into an abyss of existential emptiness, where meaning and true satisfaction become fleeting and unattainable. Instead, he suggests that we should seek a lasting good that transcends the fleeting pleasure of the senses and leads us to a higher fulfillment.

Throughout the dialogue, the discussion among the characters evolves and deepens, prompting us to consider a variety of essential philosophical concepts, such as the nature of the soul, the relationship between mind and body, and the importance of virtue. Plato urges us to explore the connection between intellect and morality, suggesting that true knowledge is intrinsically linked to virtue and righteousness. He challenges us to seek truth and wisdom not merely as ends in themselves but as means to achieve a full and virtuous life.

The dialogue *Philebus* also raises fundamental questions about the nature of language and communication. Plato invites us to question how we express and share our ideas about the good and pleasure, and how language can both be a vehicle for understanding and a barrier to truth. He explores the limitations of language and the importance of philosophy as a tool to go beyond words and reach the essence of ideas.

Ultimately, Plato's *Philebus* is a work that challenges us to explore the depths of human thought and the quest for truth. It is a work that leads us to question our own beliefs and values, inviting us to dive into philosophy as an intellectual and spiritual journey in search of the highest good. Reading this dialogue is an enriching and transformative experience, reminding us of the eternal relevance of philosophy as an unceasing pursuit of knowledge and understanding of ourselves and the world around us. *Philebus* is an invitation to deep reflection and the relentless search for truth, a work that continues to illuminate the path of philosophical inquiry, from ancient Greece to the present day.

Timaeus

"Timaeus" by Plato is a work that stands out in the seventh tetralogy of the Greek master's philosophical dialogues. In this dialogue, Plato leads us on a deep exploration of ideas regarding the creation of the universe, the nature of reality, and the nature of the human soul, engaging the reader in a fascinating intellectual journey.

The plot begins with Socrates, the main character of the dialogue, visiting the home of Timaeus, a respected mathematician and Pythagorean philosopher. From this meeting, the discussion about the origin of the universe and the intervention of a divine demiurge comes to life. Plato guides us through a meticulous line of reasoning that leads us to contemplate the harmony and order inherent in the cosmos, presenting the idea that the universe is like a great clock, designed by an intelligent creator who follows mathematical and geometric patterns. Long paragraphs are filled with detailed discussions on geometry, astronomy, and music, making the reader an active participant in this intellectual investigation.

Throughout the dialogue, Plato delves into the theory of the soul, describing it as immortal and eternal, an entity intimately linked to the demiurge and that undergoes a cycle of reincarnations. This approach provides a fascinating view of human nature and our connection with the cosmos. Through extensive paragraphs, the author reveals the idea that our quest for knowledge and truth is rooted in the nature of our soul, which seeks to unite with the world of eternal and perfect ideas.

"Timaeus" is not just a treatise on philosophy, but also an invitation to reflect on morality and ethics, inviting us to consider how the pursuit of wisdom and virtue can guide us to a more meaningful and just life. The long and engaging dialogues in this book challenge us to question our own beliefs and examine our ethical conduct.

A notable aspect of this dialogue is the way Plato unites philosophy with religion and science, seeking a unified understanding of the world. This makes "Timaeus" a rich and comprehensive work that continues to inspire scholars and readers to this day. Through long, elaborate paragraphs, Plato captivates his audience, leading us on an intellectual journey that transcends the boundaries of time and culture.

163

The richness of Plato's "Timaeus" extends beyond its metaphysical and ethical explorations, also addressing politics and education. Plato, through extensive and profound paragraphs, outlines his vision of an ideal society governed by philosopher-kings who possess deep knowledge of ideal forms and laws of justice. This political vision is intrinsically linked to the pursuit of truth and virtue. The long paragraphs serve as a vehicle to develop this philosophical utopia, which influenced political and educational thought for centuries.

Education plays a crucial role in the construction of this ideal society, with Plato arguing that education must be carefully planned to shape the minds and souls of citizens, making them capable of understanding the truth and living according to virtue. This educational vision, exposed in detail throughout the dialogue, emphasizes the importance of philosophy, music, and gymnastics in the formation of just and wise citizens. The long paragraphs unfold with a passion for knowledge and a dedication to building a society that seeks intellectual and moral excellence.

The influence of "Timaeus" on the history of philosophical and scientific thought is undeniable, with Plato addressing issues that echo in cosmology, physics, and theology throughout history. His concept of a demiurge as the creator of the universe influenced not only religious thought but also the conception of the cosmos in various cultures and philosophical traditions.

Plato's "Timaeus" challenges readers to reflect on the complexities of existence, human nature, and the relationship between man and the divine. The long, detailed paragraphs of the work invite us to dive into a sea of ideas, where abstract concepts like eternity, the soul, and the nature of knowledge are explored.

Throughout its pages, "Timaeus" leads us to reflect on the interconnection between science, philosophy, and religion, encouraging the search for knowledge and truth in all spheres of human life. Plato reminds us that philosophy is not an isolated discipline but an incessant quest to understand the complexity of the world around us and, above all, ourselves.

The interdisciplinary approach of "Timaeus" also extends to the discussion of health and medicine, with Plato highlighting the importance of harmony between the body and the soul, exploring the idea that, to achieve a state of balance and well-being, it is necessary to care for both the physical and spiritual aspects. Long, reflective paragraphs encourage us to consider how our physical health is intrinsically linked to our mental and spiritual health.

Plato's holistic view extends to his understanding of ethics and justice, arguing that justice is an extension of cosmic order, a manifestation of the harmony present in the creation of the universe. Detailed paragraphs challenge us to question our notions of right and wrong, emphasizing the importance of living according to universal ethical standards. For Plato, justice is not just a social construct but an intrinsic quality of the cosmos and the human soul.

Another notable aspect of "Timaeus" is the way Plato addresses the role of reason and language in the search for knowledge and truth, emphasizing the importance of using reason as a guide to reach a deeper understanding of reality. Long paragraphs dedicated to this issue remind us that dialogue and logical argumentation are essential tools in the pursuit of knowledge, and that philosophy is, ultimately, a collaborative effort in the search for truth.

Furthermore, "Timaeus" challenges us to consider the nature of change and permanence, suggesting that the things of the sensible world are in constant flux, but that there is an eternal and unchanging reality that we can reach through reason and reflection. Long paragraphs lead us to reflect on how change and impermanence are inherent in our experience, but that truth and eternal reality can be achieved through deep thought and contemplation.

In "Timaeus," Plato gifts us a work that transcends the boundaries of pure philosophy, permeating the essence of the human condition and existence itself. Long paragraphs carve a path that leads us to a profound reflection on the role of the human being in the vast stage of the universe. Through the character of Timaeus, Plato personifies the innate human desire to understand the origins of the world and seek a transcendental meaning in our earthly journey.

One of the most remarkable facets of "Timaeus" is its exploration of cosmology, with Plato presenting a mythological narrative of creation, where a demiurge, as a divine craftsman, molds the world from the clay of eternal ideas. This poetic and philosophical approach envelops us in a grand view of the universe, in which order, harmony, and proportion are the pillars of existence. The long paragraphs of the work lead us to a deep contemplation of the nature of reality and the relationship between the finite and the infinite, the terrestrial and the divine.

The metaphor of music also plays a crucial role in "Timaeus," with Plato inviting us to think of the cosmos as a divine symphony, where each element contributes to the harmony of the whole. The use of long, detailed paragraphs to describe this metaphor reminds us that music is a universal language that transcends cultural and linguistic barriers, uniting humanity in its search for beauty and order.

"Timaeus" also addresses the issue of the imperfection of the sensible world and the search for perfection and stability in the eternal forms, with long paragraphs exploring this concept, leading us to consider how, in the physical world, everything is subject to transformations and imperfections. But through reason and philosophy, we can seek the perfection and truth that reside in the ideal forms.

Additionally, "Timaeus" challenges us to examine the relationship between the soul and the body, shedding light on the fundamental duality that permeates human experience. It argues that the soul is immortal and eternal, while the body is mortal and transitory. The long paragraphs dedicated to this exploration lead us to a profound reflection on the nature of life, death, and the afterlife, questions that have intrigued philosophers and thinkers throughout history.

Through the dense pages of "Timaeus," Plato dives even deeper into the issue of epistemology, emphasizing that genuine knowledge must be based on beliefs grounded in reason and the search for truth. Long paragraphs, full of logical arguments and meticulous analyses, lead us through a maze of questions, prompting us to consider how knowledge is constructed, how our perceptions can deceive us, and how philosophy is an endless journey in pursuit of unreachable truth.

Moreover, the influence of mathematics and geometry in "Timaeus" is undeniable, with Plato emphasizing the importance of these disciplines as essential tools to understand the structure of the world. He describes the universe as a divine creation that follows geometric and mathematical patterns, inviting us to contemplate the deep relationship between logical thought and cosmic order.

The dialogue "Timaeus" is also an invitation to contemplate the duality of human nature, exploring how the human soul, immortal and eternal, is imprisoned in a physical body, subject to the vicissitudes of time and space. It reminds us that we are complex beings, constantly seeking balance between the demands of the body and the aspirations of the soul. Long paragraphs that address this topic guide us into a reflection on humanity's eternal struggle to transcend its physical limitations in search of meaning and purpose.

The influence of "Timaeus" on the history of philosophy and Western thought is indisputable, with its discussions on cosmology, ethics, epistemology, and human duality continuing to inspire philosophers, scientists, and thinkers worldwide. Plato's work is a testament to the capacity of philosophy to take us to new horizons of understanding and explore the most fundamental questions of existence.

In summary, Plato's "Timaeus" is a philosophical work that challenges us to explore the depths of knowledge, reality, and human nature. With long, elaborate paragraphs, Plato leads us on an intellectual journey that transcends the boundaries of time and space. This work continues to captivate and intrigue readers, stimulating the relentless pursuit of truth and wisdom. It is an intellectual beacon that illuminates the path of those who seek to unravel the mysteries of the universe and the human condition. "Timaeus" is, without a doubt, one of the greatest contributions to philosophical thought in the history of humanity.

Critias

"Critias," one of Plato's dialogues belonging to the seventh tetralogy, emerges as an intriguing and profound work that delves into the murky waters of politics, ethics, and philosophy. In this dialogue, Plato transports us to a setting marked by uncertainty and moral questions, challenging us to explore the darker corners of human nature and governance. Through a captivating narrative, filled with dialogues and meticulously crafted reflections, Plato leads us on an intellectual journey that urges us to question not only the past but also the present and future of politics and morality.

At the heart of the dialogue "Critias," we find a mythical description of the ancient Atlantis, an island believed to have been swallowed by the ocean due to its moral corruption and decay. This fascinating narrative serves as a vehicle for Plato to explore the nature of justice, virtue, and the decay of civilizations. Through the words of the character Critias, the philosopher addresses the idea that justice is a delicate and fleeting balance, which, when corrupted, can lead to the decline of an entire society.

The dialogue "Critias" challenges us to reflect on the nature of leadership and political power. While the character Critias praises the ancient Atlantis as a utopia ruled by philosopher-kings, Plato, through Socrates, questions the viability of this form of government and the ability of human beings to maintain wisdom and virtue in power. The dialogue offers a critical view of politics and the pursuit of utopia, suggesting that corruption and decay are constant threats to any society, regardless of its form of government.

The structure of the dialogue "Critias" is marked by Plato's rhetorical skill, which guides us through engaging arguments and profound philosophical inquiries. The conversations between the characters reveal the complexity of Plato's ideas, as well as his ability to explore a wide range of philosophical topics. The narrative is like a puzzle, where the reader is challenged to piece together the elements and draw conclusions about the nature of justice, morality, and politics.

One of the most striking features of the dialogue "Critias" is how Plato uses the mythical narrative of Atlantis to illustrate his philosophical ideas. The story of the fall of Atlantis serves as a powerful metaphor for the fragility of human societies and the importance of maintaining virtue and justice. Plato's ability to intertwine myth and philosophy creates a work that is both accessible and deeply reflective.

As we delve deeper into the reading of "Critias," we notice how Plato uses the figure of the wise ruler, represented by the philosopher-kings of Atlantis, as an ideal that, while unattainable in practice, represents the pursuit of a just and balanced social order. This concept prompts us to reflect on the feasibility of such governance in reality, as well as on humanity's ability to preserve ethical and moral values in positions of power. The dichotomy between the utopia of Atlantis and the imperfection of earthly politics raises profound questions about human nature and the constant struggle for social harmony.

However, "Critias" is also notable for its limitations. The work remains incomplete, which is a regrettable fact for scholars and lovers of philosophy. The abrupt interruption of the narrative leaves many questions unanswered and makes us yearn for further insights and developments. This gap in the dialogue also reminds us of the importance of uncertainty and the constant search for knowledge, an intrinsic characteristic of philosophy. Nevertheless, the legacy of "Critias" lies in what it offers us, not in what it lacks.

The influence of "Critias" throughout the history of philosophy is undeniable. The idea of a government led by philosopher-kings, though debatable and problematic in its application, continued to inspire debates about the nature of politics and justice over the centuries. Plato, through this dialogue, reminds us that the pursuit of a just and virtuous society is a constant journey and that philosophical reflection plays a key role in this pursuit.

The mythical narrative of Atlantis, with its rich description and intriguing details, is an essential part of the appeal of "Critias." It transports us to an imaginary world, full of allegories and metaphors that resonate with our understanding of the human condition. At the same time, Plato uses the story of Atlantis to explore timeless issues, such as the collapse of civilizations due to moral corruption, the struggle for power, and the inevitability of change.

In this philosophical journey in "Critias," Plato does not limit himself to presenting his vision of a society governed by philosopher-kings; he invites us to question the very concept of utopia. Atlantis, with its apparent perfection, represents an unattainable ideal, but at the same time, it makes us ask: how far can we go in our quest for a just society? To what extent can we improve our governance, our institutions, and our ethical behavior? These are questions that resonate through the centuries and continue to intrigue philosophers, politicians, and thinkers.

One of the most notable features of "Critias" is how Plato challenges us to consider the interconnection between the individual and the collective. Through his characters and dialogues, he leads us to question whether the pursuit of virtue and justice begins with the transformation of the individual or if it is a task that must be carried out together, through the reform of social and political structures. This interplay between the individual and society is a central issue in many contemporary philosophical debates, and "Critias" provides a solid foundation for deeper reflections on this topic.

Furthermore, Plato's writing in "Critias" is remarkable for its clarity and conciseness. He skillfully weaves complex arguments into accessible dialogues, making philosophy an engaging and approachable discipline for a wide range of readers. His rhetorical approach, which uses dialogue to present ideas and challenge concepts, creates an intellectually stimulating environment where readers are invited to actively participate in the quest for understanding.

It is important to emphasize that "Critias" is not just an abstract intellectual exercise, but a work that invites us to examine the society in which we live and consider how we can contribute to making it more just and virtuous. Plato urges us not only to study philosophy but also to live philosophy, to seek wisdom and apply this knowledge in our daily actions.

In a broader context, the discussion in "Critias" goes beyond the simple exploration of ideal governments and the nature of justice; it also sheds light on the role of education in the formation of virtuous citizens. Plato emphasizes the importance of an education that nurtures the soul and prepares future rulers to lead with wisdom and virtue. The idea that philosophy and education play a central role in creating ethical leaders is an issue that remains relevant today as we discuss the formation of responsible citizens and the role of education in building more just societies.

The dialogue "Critias" also takes a close look at history and memory. Atlantis is presented as an account of the past, a story that, according to Plato, was passed down from generation to generation. This leads us to reflect on how societies and civilizations construct their historical narratives and how collective memory plays a fundamental role in cultural identity. "Critias" encourages us to question the reliability of memory, distortions over time, and the meaning of history in shaping our understanding of the world.

The influence of "Critias" extends beyond the realm of philosophy; it transcends disciplinary boundaries and extends to fields such as literature, politics, and even science fiction. The narrative of Atlantis, with its advanced setting and eventual catastrophic disappearance, has inspired numerous literary works and speculations about the existence of a lost civilization. Later authors and thinkers, such as Francis Bacon and Jules Verne, were influenced by Plato's vision and explored the idea of advanced civilizations forgotten by time.

In summary, "Critias" is a work of immense philosophical richness and relevance that continues to inspire and intrigue readers across eras. Through its deep reflections, insightful dialogues, and exploration of the nature of justice, politics, and memory, Plato challenges us to think critically about the foundations of our society and the pursuit of a virtuous life. It is a work that invites us to question, explore, and venture into the complexities of the human condition and the perpetual quest for a more just and ethical world. Thus, "Critias" endures as a beacon that illuminates our ongoing search for truth, justice, and wisdom.

Laws

"Laws," the last dialogue written by Plato and part of the 7th tetralogy, is a work that takes us on a deep journey into political and moral philosophy. Often overlooked in favor of more famous works like "The Republic" or "Phaedrus," "Laws" deserves a special place in the consideration of philosophy enthusiasts. It offers a unique and insightful perspective on the nature of justice, law, and governance. As we delve into the pages of "Laws," we are invited to explore fundamental issues that echo through the centuries and remain relevant in our contemporary society.

One of the most captivating aspects of this dialogue is how Plato addresses the issue of justice. Unlike his mentor Socrates, who often explored justice in an abstract and conceptual manner, Plato in "Laws" presents us with a meticulous examination of the laws and institutions of the ideal city he proposes. He leads us to consider how justice can be embodied in the political and legal structures of society, challenging us to reflect on the practical application of ethical and moral principles in our social life, a question that remains relevant today.

The dialogue also addresses the issue of education and the formation of virtuous citizens. Plato argues that education plays a crucial role in building a just and virtuous society, discussing the importance of shaping young minds through rigorous education that instills solid moral and ethical values.

This approach resonates with current concerns about the quality of education and the formation of responsible citizens in our society, making "Laws" an insightful read for those seeking insights into the improvement of contemporary society.

Plato also explores the role of law in the governance of society, arguing that laws must be just, rational, and applied impartially. This discussion raises important questions about the rule of law, the authority of government, and the relationship between rulers and the ruled, issues that remain crucial in our current political and legal debates.

However, "Laws" is not a work that provides easy answers or definitive solutions. On the contrary, Plato challenges us to think critically about these complex issues and to seek answers through dialogue and reflection. He invites us to consider the implications of our political and moral choices and to explore what it means to live a just and virtuous life.

Plato's "Laws" stands out not only for its deep philosophical discussions but also for its practical approach to politics and governance. While many of Plato's earlier dialogues explored abstract concepts and ideals, "Laws" presents us with a vision of the ideal city shaped by laws and institutions. According to the philosopher, this city should be governed by a group of just laws rather than a monarch or aristocracy.

The emphasis on laws as the foundation of governance is a distinctive feature of this dialogue. Plato argues that, to achieve justice and harmony in society, laws must be transparent, impartial, and applied equally to all citizens. He also addresses the need for wise and adaptable laws, which can evolve with time and circumstances, demonstrating a remarkable understanding of the complexity of political life. However, Plato does not fail to recognize the complexity of human life and societies. He understands that there are no simple solutions or magic formulas for governing a just city, but he encourages us to seek a balance between principles and pragmatism. This balanced approach extends to the discussion of the nature of justice, where Plato explores the tension between the ideal and the possible, questioning whether absolute justice can be achieved in the real world.

Throughout the dialogue, Plato gifts us with a vision of education as a fundamental tool for shaping virtuous citizens. He emphasizes the importance of an education that not only imparts knowledge but also cultivates morality and ethics. This emphasis on character formation resonates deeply with our contemporary concerns about the quality of education and the need to develop responsible and ethical citizens.

Additionally, Plato's "Laws" addresses issues of religion and spirituality, showing how these elements play a vital role in the life of the ideal city. He argues that religion should be controlled by the state to ensure that it serves the interests of justice and morality. This discussion raises complex questions about the separation of church and state, religious freedom, and the authority of government over spiritual matters.

Plato's "Laws" in the 7th tetralogy is not only a philosophical treatise but also a window into the brilliant mind of the philosopher and his tireless search for truth and the improvement of society. The dialogue offers a glimpse of Plato's passion for justice, morality, and human well-being. This passion shines through in his writing, full of insightful questions and carefully crafted arguments.

One of the most notable aspects of "Laws" is the way Plato creates a vivid scenario of the ideal city, which serves as the backdrop for his discussions. He takes us on an imaginary journey through this city, detailing its laws, institutions, and daily practices. This meticulous construction of an ideal social and political environment is one of the most striking features of the work and allows us to immerse ourselves deeply in Plato's vision of how society should be structured.

The dialogue also reveals Plato's concern with human nature and the pursuit of virtue. He explores the idea that true virtue comes not only from the adherence to laws but also from the inner cultivation of the soul. This emphasis on virtue as something that goes beyond mere compliance with rules and regulations resonates in contemporary moral and ethical discussions, challenging us to consider how we can shape our own characters and improve our conduct.

Furthermore, "Laws" addresses the relationship between individual freedom and the authority of the state. Plato acknowledges the need for a strong government to maintain order and ensure justice but also warns against tyranny and oppression. This discussion strongly resonates with current political debates on the balance between individual freedom and state authority, a topic that remains central in today's democratic societies. Plato challenges us to think not only about political and legal structures but also about the importance of education, morality, and religion in the formation of a just society. He reminds us that the pursuit of justice and virtue should be a collective effort involving not only institutions but also individuals and culture at large.

Ultimately, Plato's "Laws" is a work rich in insights and reflections that remain relevant and captivating. The dialogue invites us to explore complex and timeless issues, challenging us to consider how we can apply Plato's philosophical principles in our own pursuit of a just society and a virtuous life. It is a reading that rewards the inquisitive mind and takes us on a deep intellectual journey, where the fundamental questions of justice, morality, and governance are explored with clarity of thought and depth of vision that make Plato one of the greatest philosophers in history.

Final Notes:

This compendium was created with the goal of making Plato's Seven Tetralogies more accessible and understandable, offering an analysis that simplifies, without losing depth, the philosophical concepts that Plato presents in his works. We know that these works can often seem complex and challenging, but the intention of this book is to bring the reader closer to the richness and relevance of these philosophical discussions for modern thought.

Each dialogue has been carefully dissected and explained in a way that any reader, even without a deep prior knowledge of philosophy, can grasp the fundamental ideas and reflect on their implications. By making Plato's philosophy more accessible, we aim not only for a clearer understanding but also for an enriching experience that encourages continuous reflection on topics such as justice, ethics, knowledge, and the nature of reality.

We thank you for embarking on this philosophical journey and hope that this compendium has fulfilled its mission of shedding light, in a simple and direct way, on Plato's timeless ideas. May your reflections inspire new questions, new thoughts, and, perhaps, new paths of wisdom.

Bibliographic references:

ALTMAN, Sam. OpenAI. Available at: https://openai.com/brand/. Accessed on: January 23, 2025.

CONTRA OS ACADÊMICOS, 2022. Contra os acadêmicos: ordered reading list: Plato. Available at: https://contraosacademicos.com.br/public/biblioteca/lista-de-leitura-ordenada-platao. Accessed on: January 23, 2025.

FELLER, José Nunes. (2003). JOSÉ NUNES FELLER CHARITABLE GROUP. Available at: https://www.grupofeller.com.br/single-post/2018/07/08/plat%C3%A3o. Accessed on: January 23, 2025.

OPENAI. ChatGPT. (2022). Available at: https://chatgpt.com/?model=auto. Accessed on: January 23, 2025.

PERKINS, Melanie. CANVA, (2025). Available at: https://www.canva.com/pt_br/. Accessed on: January 23, 2025.

VYRO LLC. IMAGINE AI, (2022). Available at: https://imagine.art/. Accessed on: January 23, 2025.

Please be aware that these texts were partially generated by artificial intelligence and implemented in most of the work presented in this compendium. The citation of the logo and the respective name of the company OpenAI ("OpenAI, ChatGPT") is properly displayed on the cover or on the first pages of the book, along with the logo and the respective name of the publisher and distributor

Don't miss out!

Visit the website below and you can sign up to receive emails whenever Rodrigo v. santos publishes a new book. There's no charge and no obligation.

https://books2read.com/r/B-A-ULDBB-GNBUF

BOOKS 2 READ

Connecting independent readers to independent writers.

Also by Rodrigo v. santos

Compêndios da filosofia
Friedrich Nietzsche: Como a filosofia molda a ambição humana
Platão: como a filosofia molda a compreensão humana
George Hegel: Como a filosofia molda a consciência humana

Philosophical compendiums
Friedrich Nietzsche: How Philosophy Shapes Human Ambition
Plato: How Philosophy Shapes Human Understanding.